SURVIVING
TEENAGERS

Little children – headache; big children – heartache.

(Italian proverb)

SURVIVING TEENAGERS

Dr David Fong

GEDDES &
GROSSET

Published 2007 by Geddes & Grosset
David Dale House, New Lanark, ML10 9DJ, Scotland

© Geddes & Grosset 2007

Text by David Fong
Illustrations supplied by Domex India

ISBN 10: 1 84205 570 4

ISBN 13: 978 1 84205 570 0

Printed and bound in Poland

POLSKABOOK

Dedication

This book is dedicated to my family and friends who gave me the inspiration to come back to the UK, rent a flat I couldn't afford, receive armfuls of rejection letters from publishers and end up back where I started instead of taking the job on the beach in Sicily. Thanks, guys!

About the author

Dr David Fong qualified as a clinical psychologist in 1997 and then worked with children, adolescents and families in Sheffield. A three-month sabbatical abroad developed into a three-year journey, during which he visited fifteen different countries, taught English in Italy for two years and wrote *Not Another Self-help Book*, published in 2005 by Geddes and Grosset. He has written more than twenty-five articles on mental health for the magazine *My Weekly*, busked in Japan, New Zealand and Venice, played drums in various bands, can't swim and counts among his major achievements learning how to ride a push bike at the age of twenty-seven.

Contents

Introduction

Are you having problems with your teenage child(ren)?

Are they causing you hair loss, sleepless nights and doubts over your own sanity?

Are you looking back with rose-tinted glasses to those halcyon days when all you had to worry about was changing a nappy?

Are you feeling as if you need someone to translate what your teenager is saying to you?

Do you feel like you need some down-to-earth and practical advice and information?

If you have answered 'yes' to some or all of these questions, then welcome to this book . . . you're in the right place.

This slim volume is crammed with useful advice and suggestions to make home a more harmonious place to live. It will explain what you can and cannot expect from a teenager and, just as importantly, what a teenager can expect from their parents. This book will explain what is and what isn't normal about those tricky teenage years and also look at the feelings and stresses that affect both adolescents and their parents.

Parenting and growing up are both very stressful things to be doing and when a family is trying to do them both at the same time, it's inevitable that somewhere along the line there is going to be friction. But friction doesn't have to lead to rifts; a shared understanding of what is going on at home can drastically improve how happy a family feels.

This book is aimed primarily at the parents of adolescents, but also presents a teenager's point of view as well. With the benefit of twenty-twenty hindsight I can honestly state that not only did I make cringeworthy mistakes myself as a teenager (and after that, too), but my parents dropped a few clangers as well. This is perfectly normal; parents who want either to be perfect themselves or to have perfect adolescents who never make mistakes should put this book down and try somewhere else (and if you find the secret of perfection, do write and let me know what it is).

The book presents useful information in an easy-to-digest way as well as helping parents to clarify not only what they do well but also what they don't do so well and how that can be improved. The book will look at the different pressures – psychological, social, physical, emotional and behavioural – that adolescents are under, as well as looking at ways for parents to handle each. It will debunk some of the myths about adolescents and the world they live in as well as some of the myths about 'perfect parenting'. In short, the book will act as a mine of information as well as a small but perfectly formed little helper in times of stress.

So without further ado, let's get on with it!

Chapter 1 More like the Waltons and less like the Simpsons

What is normal anyway?

Normal?

Before we think about the problems that families and adolescents have, we first need to think about families and what can be considered as normal – which is harder than it looks!

Normal?

Normal?

That paragon of common sense, George Bush Senior, famously remarked in 1992 that he wanted American families to be 'more like the Waltons and less like the Simpsons.'

By this, he implied that what was normal and good for a family was:

- to be toothpaste-commercial happy

- to be always in harmony – no fighting or disagreements

- to have siblings who never argued and who sailed through adolescence without the slightest hint of hormonal imbalance

- to always have happy endings.

On the other hand, it would be bad for a family to be like the Simpsons:

- arguing

- fighting

- struggling and making endless mistakes

- strangling each other (well, perhaps that is bad).

Bush's comments (and remember, George Senior is supposed to be the smart one) were met with hoots of laughter from both sides of the Atlantic. Why?

Because the idea that family life should be nothing but harmonious bliss is, and excuse the technical term, absolute bunkum. Family life exists on a line or continuum. Sometimes, it's absolutely great and sometimes, well, it really isn't. Relationships of all kinds have their ebbs and flows, their ups and downs, their good points and their bad points. No son or daughter is perfect and neither are their parents. If all families were made to stand on this continuum, with the Simpsons at one end and the Waltons at the other, most families would be somewhere in the middle. Furthermore, it is important to bear in mind that where a family sits on this line varies according to the stresses and strains they are under.

So first of all, reassure yourself that no matter what is happening to your family, no matter what is going on both for you and your offspring:

You are not alone!

What Bush also failed to take into consideration is the fact that families don't pop into existence out of nowhere and then stay the same forever. A family is part of a community, which is part of a village, which is part of a district . . . and so on. There is a huge interaction between a family, its members and their environment and things are changing all the time. So let's take a quick look at how these interactions have influenced what can be considered 'normal'.

2.4 kids?

Let's have a look at some facts and figures. Back in the 1950s, to have a child outside marriage was considered to be an act of almost unmentionable shamefulness. Women who had children without husbands were thought to be morally lacking in some way, which is probably why only about four per cent of all children born during this decade were born outside wedlock. By the year 2000, however, this proportion was up to forty per cent.

In the year 2000, nearly twenty per cent of children lived with their mother only, a figure that would have been unimaginable in the 1950s. Divorce rates today, aided by 'quickie' divorces, suggest that almost one in three children born to married parents witness their parents divorcing before the age of sixteen. As recently as the 1970s, mixed marriages, blending people from different cultures, were rare and often regarded with blunt hostility and suspicion if they did happen (some would say this hasn't changed, but mixed race families are far more common). Even though it is still often the case that fathers go to work and mothers stay home with the children, the concept of both parents working and even that of the 'house husband' have now become common and accepted as normal.

In other words, the idea of a 'typical' family has changed beyond belief in an amazingly short period of time. The 'normal' family structure has changed, the composition of a 'typical' family has changed, everything's changing! So, the second point to remember is this – there shouldn't be any shame attached to the way your family is made up. If you are a single mother of two mixed-race adolescents, or a couple looking after children from different marriages, or a single dad raising his children:

None of these things are weird or abnormal.

The characteristics of successful families

So if we don't know what's normal,
how can we tell if we have a problem?

I'm very glad you asked. Although families can be put together in lots of different ways and although their offspring come in infinite shapes and sizes, there are lots of things that psychologically successful families have in common. Although it is true to say that family composition has changed out of all recognition in the last fifty years, what a family needs to do hasn't changed that much. In other words, there are characteristics of families that psychologists see as being 'good things' that are shared by families that report being happy and who seem to do well, not in terms of earning fat wodges of cash and driving around in Mercedes, but in terms of contentment, adjustment and coping strategies. This list is not exhaustive, nor should you worry if your family is not doing all of these things all of the time. As I mentioned earlier, families change.

The characteristics of psychologically successful families are related directly to how well they undertake the tasks required to meet the triangle of needs shown below. Most families successfully do the tasks at the bottom but the further up the triangle you go, the more complicated the task becomes.

The triangle of needs

9

Physical needs

At the bottom of the triangle are the tasks associated with our basic physical needs and the successful family provides food, shelter, warmth and clothing for its members. In other words, it gets all the physical basics right: a warm, clean place to live, adequate food and nutrition, and clothing. Even with the best will in the world, if you're living in a rat-infested shed at the bottom of a quarry with nothing to eat, you're going to be concentrating on keeping Mr and Mrs Rat out of your cornflakes, rather than the psychological development of your family.

Psychological needs

The family also provides for the psychological needs of its members. These needs are slightly more complex. A successful family needs to make all its members feel psychologically safe. Imagine a mother who tells her children 'If you misbehave, I'm leaving!' Statements such as this will make it very difficult for her children to feel psychologically safe and they may be prone to anxiety and its flip side, depression. But it is not just the children in the family who need to feel psychologically safe. Parents need to feel that they can rely on their partners to be there for them and support them. Again, imagine a husband telling his wife that he's thinking of going to work in Japan for two years and leaving her and the kids behind. It will be very difficult for his wife to feel settled and confident, which will obviously have an impact on how she parents their children.

As well as safety, a family needs to provide what psychologists refer to as 'a secure base'. Imagine an elastic band that stretches around all the members of a family. This elastic band enables all the family members to feel attached to one another and they can all explore and do different things, safe in the knowledge that they have a home, not just in the physical sense, but also in the psychological sense. Imagine the effects on a child if this elastic band snaps too early and they are left to fend for themselves at an early age before they have had time to develop as a person; for that child, the world can become a dangerous and unpredictable place.

Now imagine that a child is not given any freedom and the elastic band acts as a restraint. This child grows up unprepared for the challenges of the world outside the family unit and unable to fend for itself. Getting the lengths and durability of these elastic bands right is a major task for every family. A successful family provides a happy balance – an elastic band that is neither too restrictive nor too free.

Emotional needs

As successful families grow together, they create what can be thought of as emotional and behavioural thermostats that provide appropriate limits to the emotions within the family. The parents in a family have to teach their children that emotions are not bad things and allow their children to be angry, sad, miserable and so on. However, all families have to have limits and boundaries to these emotions. If a child learns from their father, for example, that the best way to deal with the emotion of anger is to hit someone or run off to the pub and get drunk, that father cannot complain when his teenager goes out and gets into trouble with the police for antisocial behaviour. The successful family acts as both an emotional and a behavioural thermostat, ensuring that the emotional needs of the family are met within appropriate boundaries and limits.

Furthermore, children have to develop behavioural repertoires. If a brother steals their Playstation game, a child learns that an appropriate response is to ask for it back and if this is refused then to tell someone in authority. The child needs to learn that hitting their brother in the face or pushing them down the stairs is not an appropriate response. Families develop these thermostats as time goes on. The best thermostats are the ones that kick in when the behaviour or the emotional response becomes inappropriate or even dangerous to the wellbeing of family members.

Spiritual needs

The family also allows for the meeting of spiritual needs. By this, I don't mean that the family should train its members to be priests or nuns. What I do mean is that if all of the other needs of a family are met, then the family members can dream, have ambitions and goals beyond their material and emotional needs. They can feel spiritually fulfilled and experience an almost indefinable sense of wellbeing and belonging.

I have to admit that this is more of an ideal thing – I haven't met a family yet that manages to live in this state all of the time!

Emotional thermostats, rubber bands and other family functions

Now, be honest, did you have any idea that the things that families do for each other are so incredibly complex – that what a family provides for its members psychologically, emotionally and all those other words ending in '-ally', can be seen as an

14

incredibly complex spider web, balancing everyone's needs in a finely tuned world that takes years to create?

You did? Well, then, let me ask you another question:

> Given how complex families are, is it any
> wonder that sometimes things go wrong?

We have moved around a lot in this chapter (and it's only the first!) in an attempt to demonstrate two key points:

1. The idea of a typical family has changed enormously over the years.

Families interact with the world they exist in and no one should feel ashamed if their family doesn't appear to be 'typically typical'.

It's important to remember that because families are always changing and evolving, there is always room to try different things.

15

2. Families are monstrously complicated things.

Successful families have a number of characteristics that centre on the way they meet various needs. These needs are met with varying degrees of success, depending on what is going on for a family at the time.

Before we go on, it is necessary (for me at least!) to simplify things a bit. We are going to talk about adolescents really soon, I promise, but it's important to remember that adolescents don't exist in a vacuum (even though I'm sure there are times when you wish they would) and we need a bit of context. There is another thing that all families do all of the time and it can be handy to bear it in mind. What is it?

They create meaning.

What does this mean? Well . . . everyday is different. It is really difficult to predict how each new day is going to go and what is going to happen. Picture a family of a mum, a dad and a child. Everyday, Dad takes little Janey to school. By doing this, Dad creates his day, his identity. He is a father taking his daughter to school and out of all the millions of things that he could be doing, he has chosen to do this. This action gives his life meaning.

Little Janey is also creating meaning for herself. She is learning, growing, developing, making friends. When Mum and Dad ask her, 'How was school today?' and she is able to give them an answer, this is because Janey has also created a meaning for her day.

Now, while Janey is at school, Mum is cleaning the house, seeing friends and preparing to go and pick Janey up from school. All these things give meaning to Mum's day. They are different meanings from Dad's and Janey's but when the family is together, all of these meanings make sense and can be shared.

Therefore, as well as all the other things that we mentioned earlier, families create meanings for their members as well as a shared meaning that helps to write the family's individual and unique story.

That's all very well and good, but . . . OK, thank you for your patience. I have finally arrived at my point. We have seen how complex families and their functions are. We have seen how these functions all go towards creating a shared story for the family. Now . . .

Imagine that you introduce into this family someone who has a totally different behavioural and emotional thermostat; who has totally different norms of behaviour; who stretches the elastic band until it's almost at snapping point and then lets go; who has no real idea of what meanings they want to create, but is very sure that they don't want the meanings that their parents and siblings have. Who or what is this rampant, out of control monster?

It's your teenager!

Chapter 2
Be afraid, very afraid!

They aren't monsters, really

Poor adolescents. They aren't monsters, really. But the number of times I have heard this expression, both in clinical situations and from friends (and from my parents, come to think of it), suggests that it is a fairly common lament. And there is some truth in this lament – if you think about the word 'monster', what do you think about? Perhaps Frankenstein, vampires, the Hulk, aliens – often creatures who shift from one form to another. During the teenage years, this is pretty much what happens. There are enormous changes for a teenager, physically, emotionally, psychologically and behaviourally during adolescence.

We'll look at all of these, the problems they cause for the family and for the teenagers themselves, as well as looking at strategies to help ensure as smooth a ride as possible. After all, that's why you've picked up this slim tome instead of the one on runes.

First let's look take a look at the three terms that are most frequently used to describe this time in your child's life in Information Point 1 on the next page.

Then join me as we take a very short tour through the changing body of a teenager. Hold on tight, because it's a really bumpy ride!

INFORMATION POINT 1

A brief glossary

puberty

the period in a young person's life in which sexual development occurs. At the end of this period, the person is physically capable of reproduction and has undergone numerous physical changes. This period can start as early as eight in girls and as late as thirteen; for boys, it tends to be a little bit later, starting between the ages of around nine to fourteen.

adolescence

the period between childhood and adulthood – the word 'adolescence' comes from a Latin term and literally means 'to grow into maturity'. Adolescence is broadly divided into three stages: early adolescence (very roughly between the ages of nine and thirteen) is characterised by the onset of puberty and the rise in importance of a peer group; middle adolescence (again, very roughly between fourteen and seventeen) is characterised

by early romantic attachments and deeper friend-
ships, but also by risk-taking behaviour and
boundary testing; while late adolescence (between
the ages of eighteen and the early twenties) is
characterised by the development of longer-term
goals. These age bands are very approximate and
some adolescents take longer than others to reach
maturity.

teenage

the chronological period between the ages of
thirteen and nineteen.

I tend to use the word 'adolescent' in this book
because some of the things that I'll be talking about
happen before the age of thirteen or carry on after
the age of nineteen. Psychologists can be really picky
can't they?

The biology of it all

There are a number of key physical changes that
happen to everyone (males and females) during
puberty. The significance of these changes is
secondary only to the changes that occur during the

first two years of life and they affect every system in the body. Let's look at these in turn, and apologies if the next part of the book is a little bit dry!

Growth occurs and the body starts to change

Simply put, during puberty, the body gets bigger and starts to develop more adult characteristics. Legs start to lengthen, followed by the trunk and there can be a dramatic growth spurt (as much as four or five inches of height in a year). It's easy to see why some adolescents can be clumsy – imagine reaching for a cup on a table and finding out your arms are a couple of inches longer than they used to be!

Muscles start to develop and bones start to harden. Girls put down more fat deposits and have a higher ratio of fat to muscle. During puberty, girls start to develop the typically curvy feminine shape as fat is laid down around the breasts, buttocks and hips. Boys start to develop the typical 'male' shape; shoulders broaden and the neck becomes more muscular. The external male genitalia – the penis and testicles – start to grow, as does the vagina in girls.

23

During adolescence, there are other important physical changes, such as boys developing a deeper voice as the voice box changes. This can cause an embarrassing 'cracking' of the voice, as the high-pitched tones of a child start to take on deeper, more adult characteristics before they finally settle.

Boys also develop facial hair and start to need to shave. Body hair increases and can be found on the back, legs and chest. Pubic hair starts to grow in both girls and boys as well as underarm hair. Unfortunately, as underarm hair grows and develops, so do the sweat glands (leading to the development of body odour) and the oil glands in the skin (leading to acne).

Sexual characteristics begin to develop

The sexual changes that happen in puberty are usually divided into primary and secondary characteristics. The secondary characteristics have been mentioned above – they are the ones that make it possible to distinguish between boys and girls – for example, the development of breasts in girls, the enlargement of the penis and the testicles descending in boys.

The primary sexual characteristics are not as obvious to see, but are extremely important. In girls, the menarche begins. Hormonal changes (and more about hormones later) lead to the first period, when the lining of the uterus is shed and appears outside the body as menstrual blood. This process of menstruation really marks the beginning of a girl's sexual life, in the sense that her body is now capable of carrying a baby.

In boys, the spermache begins, where the male reproductive system produces sperm and the ability to ejaculate this through the penis. The ability to produce healthy sperm means that the boy is now capable of impregnating a female.

It should be noted at this point that although males and females are physically capable of creating life together at this point in their development, they may not be ready psychologically, emotionally, financially or behaviourally to parent a child in the modern world.

For our ancestors, there was no question of 'Let's wait until we're ready to have a child.' It was a case of 'Let's reproduce like rabbits' because the chances of children surviving were not great. In today's world, although the chances of having your offspring killed by a woolly mammoth are pretty slim, there are other far more subtle dangers to a child's wellbeing that must be taken into account before people conceive. It can be monumentally difficult for a young person who has not progressed that far through their own development to attempt to carry another individual through theirs.

Hormonal changes

Our bodies are full of hormones – chemicals that are responsible for triggering certain effects in different parts of the body. Well known hormones include adrenaline, which triggers the 'fight or flight' reflex in a dangerous situation, and melatonin, which triggers our sleep/wake cycle. They are carried through the body in body fluids and there is an absolute explosion of them during puberty.

In girls, the most powerful and predominant hormone at this stage is oestrogen. Secreted by the female's ovaries, this hormone is transported to the different parts of the body and is responsible for the changes in the physical characteristics of the female. Oestrogen is also partly responsible for emotional development and control. So as well as being vital for all the physical changes that a pubertal female goes through, it is linked to the moodiness, emotional outbursts and tendency towards low mood that are frequently seen in female adolescents – hence, the age-old cry:

Her hormones are going crazy!

In males, the most powerful hormone is testosterone. As the male's testicles develop, they secrete testosterone. This hormone is taken to various parts of the body and is responsible for the growth and the development of those secondary sexual characteristics. But as the male grows and develops, hormones are also responsible for the development and regulation of emotion. The characteristic mood outbursts, aggression and temper flare ups seen in adolescent boys seem to be caused by these hormones – hence the other age-old cry:

He's a mass of hormones at the moment!

I must say that that was an ultra-brief whiz through the physical changes that a teenager goes through – entire books can be found just explaining the biology of these changes! But try this little thought experiment for a while, just to put yourself in your teenager's shoes.

THOUGHT EXPERIMENT 1

However old you are and whatever you're doing in life at the moment, imagine that over the next three or four years . . .

- you sprout hair all over your body

- your voice changes completely

- your body odour changes

- you find that you can't judge distance because your limbs are growing

- you have strange urges that you've never had before

- you can't seem to control your mood because your body is awash with hormones

- your sex organs start behaving in strange ways and there are bodily fluids coming from every orifice

. . . and to top it off, everyone around starts saying things like 'Well, you have to make decisions that will influence the rest of your life from now on! You're much more adult now! But don't forget to do your Maths homework, take your little brother to the swings for the afternoon and don't forget to take out the garbage!'

The impact of physical changes on a teenager

These physical changes in early adolescence can be incredibly confusing. For a child, the years between about three and ten are marked by fairly subtle changes that are relatively continuous (that is, less abrupt and sudden than the changes in adolescence) and often in a school class of thirty pupils, there can be not that much to tell all the pupils apart.

Before . . .

. . . After

But early adolescence and puberty leads to the development of obvious changes and they do not happen in a social vacuum.

Developing breasts can be very embarrassing for girls if they are early starters and one of the few in the class to have them and it can be just as embarrassing if they are a late developer and so feel

31

excluded. Having their first period can be frightening and embarrassing and, for some girls, even shameful if they have not been told about the changes that will occur. Girls in a social group can often be quite cutting in their remarks to other girls, which can further isolate already vulnerable individuals.

As boys develop physically, the competitive edge that has always existed between them can take on a darker tone. Late physical maturers can be seen as 'wimps' or somehow inadequate.

The role of peer groups becomes progressively more important during these times and can often be regarded as 'the blind leading the blind'.

Adolescents taking their first steps towards independence and going through countless physical changes that are often associated with shame and embarrassment (and hence are not talked about calmly and rationally) often take advice from their peers, who are just as badly informed as they are.

Hence, the typical emotional consequences of the physical changes that adolescents go through can involve any one of, or a combination of:

- embarrassment and shame

- awkwardness and confusion

- fear and depression.

What can be done to help?

As I mentioned above, the physical changes that occur in adolescence do not happen in a vacuum. This is an important point that we will keep revisiting until everybody is heartily sick of it.

For the child of seven or eight, their world really consists of their parents, their siblings and their school and school friends – pretty much in that order of importance, too. For the adolescent, their peer group, interactions with members of the opposite sex, the wider world outside home and school, parents, siblings, teachers, rapid physical, emotional and psychological change – all interact, moulding and shaping the individual into the adult they will become. The environment at home, though, is still vitally important; friends will come and go, but family will always be family.

We will look at some of the effects on family life a little bit later, once we know exactly what we are dealing with. But when it comes to handling the physical changes that a teenager goes through, what can be done? Here are some suggestions.

- Be sensitive.

Jokes about an adolescent's appearance can backfire horribly. Whether you have a teenage son or daughter, what might be harmless joshing to a parent can feel like being hit over the head with a brick to a teenager.

Compliment your teenager; they may react with 'Oh, please', but the compliment will be registered somewhere. Treat the external physical changes in your children with understanding, helping your adolescent daughter with her first bra, your adolescent son with his first razor and can of deodorant.

• Be informed.

Nothing will cause an adolescent to seek out bad information more than badly informed parents. If you feel embarrassed and nervous about talking about periods with your teenage daughter then she will learn that they are something to be embarrassed and nervous about.

Males tend to be lousy at talking about anything sexual without giggling but it is important for adolescent males to know that there is a time to be serious about it and a time to joke. It may be that fathers need to be honest about the physical changes that occur, even down to talking about wet dreams (dreams that occur during the night with strong sexual themes that often lead to the adolescent's first ejaculation) and masturbation.

Be ready to talk about things that may seem far too

'adult' to be discussing with someone who, five years ago, only wanted to talk about 'My Little Pony' or 'Power Rangers'. Leave information about the physical changes in adolescence, such as a book like this or information from an organisation such as Brook (see page 211), around the house so that they can be read and picked through by your adolescent.

• Normalise.

There is a classic moment in the film *Teen Wolf* where Michael J. Fox is standing in the bathroom, looking in horror at the bathroom mirror as he slowly turns into a werewolf. As his father bangs on the door asking him what's wrong, the Teen Wolf says 'I'm just going through some . . . changes.' When the hirsute teen shamefully opens the door, he finds his equally hirsute father standing there. 'Tell me about it,' his father says!

It's important for adolescents to know that all the physical changes that they are going through are normal and that, weird though it may seem, Mum and Dad have gone through them too. They are not going mad, they are not deformed, they are simply changing and their body is being prepared for their adulthood.

• Be prepared.

The physical changes that occur in adolescence do bring consequences. Clumsiness may be a part of this, as well as experimentation with different styles of hair and dress. There will be the expense of buying clothes that are absolute 'must-haves' today and totally out of date tomorrow. Giving an adolescent their own budget for clothes and accessories can be a useful way of introducing the idea of buying thriftily with your own money instead of wildly extravagantly with someone else's!

• Be open and accepting.

As adolescents find out more and more about themselves, some adolescents realise that their sexuality is not geared towards members of the opposite sex, but towards their own. It should be noted that many people who describe their sexual orientation as heterosexual have had homosexual experiences – as many as one in three men and women have had such experiences.

Therefore, these experiences, in the context of social experimentation, do not necessarily dictate a person's sexual orientation for the rest of their life (see Information Point 2 on sexual orientation on the next page).

- Keep out of 'the Bat Cave'.

It may be because of the physical changes that adolescents go through or the psychological ones or a combination of many different things, but virtually all adolescents develop an increased need for privacy and personal space. It can be difficult for parents to accept that just a few years ago, little Janey loved it when Daddy burst into her room to play horsey or little Freddy couldn't restrain his enthusiasm for the next game of football – but now, the only riposte parents get is randomly aimed books and shoes while being screamed at to:

Leave me alone!

Parents must respect this private space as well as acknowledging that a teenager's personal bubble can vary in size depending on mood from a few inches to several miles.

Agree what the rules and boundaries are with your adolescent; this can be an important lesson in negotiation for all membersof the family and can help prevent 'You-were-in-my-room-weren't-you-why-can't-you-learn-to-respect-my-privacy-oh-God-I-hate-you' conversations.

INFORMATION POINT 2

Sexual orientation

Adolescent sexuality is confusing enough without fearing the prejudice and hostility that comes from other people's ignorance – can you believe that thirty-five years ago, homosexuality was listed as a 'mental disorder'?

Adolescents who are confused about their sexuality

often find that the burden of this worry can be terrible – they need someone to talk to and they need that person to be judgement free.

It is important for adolescents who think that their sexual orientation may be different from their peers:

• to be heard without prejudice.

Parents often feel very worried for the children in terms of the prejudices that other people have and often find that they have prejudices of their own that they hadn't realised.

• to feel that they are not alone.

In today's world, there isn't the same degree of hostility against homosexuality as there was, although there is no question that prejudice does still exist. However, organisations do exist to support people worried about their sexuality, such as the following website:

http://www. queeryouth.org.uk

This website has a confidential 'Agony Uncle' who can answer questions or queries. Another useful website can be found at:

http://www.cyh.com

This is the service for Young Adult Health in Australia and has a variety of excellent advice for adolescents on a variety of topics, including 'coming out'. There are also some good articles here for parents.

- to feel that their family accepts them.

Sexuality is one part of a person's make up, not all of it. An adolescent who has been honest and open about their sexuality needs to know that their family accepts them forwhat they are, whether that be homosexual, heterosexual or bisexual.

What goes on in the mind of your teenager?

Phew! OK, everybody, take a deep breath. It's tricky stuff, adolescence, isn't it? And that's just some of the external physical changes we've talked about.

Of course, there are also all the things that aren't so obvious – all the stuff that goes on inside the mind of a teenager – and the changes that go on in there are just as profound. Let me be your guide in the next chapter as we take a trip through the internal world of a teenager.

Chapter 3
What's going on in there?

Adolescence begins when children stop asking
questions – because they know all the answers.
(Evan Esar, American author and humourist)

The psychology of it all

I hope you've recovered from that little tour around
your teenager's changing body. And all those changes
happening in such a phenomenally short period of
time! It's no wonder adolescents can have short fuses.
Let's think now about all the changes that go on inside
the teenager's mind. Because this is a short book, I'm
afraid that I'm going to have throw everyone in at the
deep end with some fairly complex ideas, but I'll do my
best to keep it all relevant. OK . . . ready?

Everybody has two worlds, the internal and the
external. The external world is the stuff that we
can really see. School, family relationships, peer
relationships, jobs, hobbies and interests. Driving all
of these external things is the internal world, which
for many people is even more complex. The internal

world comprises our feelings (or emotions), our thoughts (or cognitions), our hopes, dreams and ambitions. In our internal world, we plan on the future, reflect on the past and exist in the present. We test our ideas, rehearse conversations with people, imagine ourselves in different roles. Behind our exterior appearance, there's a whole other reality going on.

It's important to note at this point that a very important factor that shapes both our internal and external realities is choice. All the way through our lives, we must make choices and these choices influence both of our realities. We have to make choices . . .

because

it's impossible to do everything

because

we're not going to live forever.

Imagine this – your life has been nurtured and shaped by your parents. A lot of your ideas, whether you like it or not, are your parents' ideas. Many of your interests will have been shaped by your parents' interests, as will many of your attitudes. All of a sudden, you realise that you want your own interests, your own ideas, your own attitudes. The problem is this: your parents have had a vast amount of experience shaping these things for themselves, so where do you start where you're only twelve years old?

As we saw in Chapter 2, there are a huge number of different physical changes that a teenager must go through. The psychological changes that occur – the ones that go on inside a person's internal world – are just as profound, complex and wide reaching. We'll look at some of the key ones in this chapter:

- choice and consequence

- separation and individuation

- development of a stable internal model

- emotional regulation.

Choice and consequence

A - LEVELS OR WORK?
JASON OR JENNY?
HOME OR UNI?
TATTOOS OR A - LINE SKIRT?

So many choices and so many decisions!

We all make choices everyday and each and every choice has its consequences. Deciding to have coffee with our morning toast is a choice. The consequences of this choice are: firstly, we have made a decision to not have tea, water or anything else;

secondly, we may feel a bit jittery for an hour or so; and thirdly, that we may need to visit the toilet more often. It's a choice that we can make without a lot of thought or effort. But we make bigger decisions, too – we decide to go for that job and not this job; we decide to be with that person and not this person; we decide to have children – a decision that will have all manner of consequences, many of which are impossible to predict. But the ability to make these decisions comes from our life experience.

How do we learn to make decisions?

For a child, the choices that they have to make are not usually very wide reaching in terms of their consequences. A ten-year-old child may feel disappointment at Christmas that they asked for (and received) a Playstation, when they realise what they really wanted after all was an X-Box. They may feel chastised when the consequences of kicking their little brother during a football game involve no sweeties after tea and an early night.

47

Children learn and are taught a variety of consequences for their behaviour, in the shape of a simple equation:

If I do 'x' then 'y' will happen. Is it worth it?

This simple equation is hugely important because within it the seeds of being able to delay gratification and predict outcomes are sown.

For the adolescent, the choices suddenly mushroom, as do the many consequences. The world becomes highly unpredictable, because a lot of the choices that adolescents make are being made for the first time.

Here is a classic example:

Ask any adult what happens to them if they drink ten pints of beer (action 'x'). Some adults will say 'I'll fall over and be sick.' Some will say, 'I never drink ten pints, I always stop at four.' Others will say, 'I prefer wine.' Ask a fourteen-year-old what will happen if they drink ten pints of beer and they won't know.

They may be able to imagine what will happen, but it's all guesswork. Adults have learnt (or should have anyway) that action 'x' (drinking ten pints of beer) has certain consequences. They then make a decision or choice about those consequences and from that decision comes a course of action.

There are a number of questions that we all ask ourselves subconsciously when we make a decision – but look how hard these questions are to answer for an adolescent.

• What do I know about this situation and what information do I need to make an informed choice?

Adolescents are often making decisions about things for the first time without an experience base to guide them, so where can they find the information they need? They might try their peers, who probably haven't done the thing they want information about either; or their parents who, they are starting to realise, don't know it all; or the TV or media, a mass of conflicting information aimed at selling things; or the government who seem to give conflicting advice depending on who's speaking and whether or not there's an election coming up.

- What will be the consequences?

Well, how do you know the consequences of an action until you do it? How do you predict consequences on the basis of really wobbly information? It's very difficult to judge the costs and benefits of an action when you've never done something before. And all of a sudden, the consequences can be irrevocable and serious – the ten-year-old child who chose the PlayStation over the X-Box can always save some money or ask for the X-Box for their birthday; four years later, they could be trying to make a decision over whether or not to keep a baby.

How parents can help

Parents clearly have a very important role to play in helping their adolescent son or daughter to make the right choices and there are two things that they can do to make sure that they have done the best they can.

1. Parents need to be honest and available.

Don't force your decisions on your teenager. One of the most difficult things for parents to accept is that their children are going to make decisions of their own, about their boyfriends and girlfriends, clothes, music and friends. Parents have to strike a new balance; instead of telling their children what to do, they must guide their children by giving advice in a nonjudgemental way and by explaining why they are giving this advice. Parents must also be prepared for their children not to take their advice and then be available to console and support in the event of negative consequences. Learn this rule and learn it well:

Adolescents will screw up!

And when they do, they will feel bad enough about it without having their Mum or Dad yelling at them for being 'bloody irresponsible'.

2. Parents need to set boundaries.

Adolescents will test boundaries. This is another

instance when a new balance has to be struck. Just as adolescents are making it all up as they go, so parents have to accept that they too are in uncharted territory. But you do have more experience than they do! While you must accept that adolescents will make some decisions that you wouldn't make yourself, you must also draw a line under what is and what isn't acceptable.

For example, many adolescents experiment with smoking; as a parent, you may accept this but you tell your teenager that smoking is not acceptable in the house, explain the health risks and why you don't want them to start. Telling a teenager that if they dare to smoke then they had better pack their bags and go do it somewhere else merely reinforces for a teenager a) that smoking is something rebellious and cool and b) that they can't have a conversation with their parents.

The boundaries that you set for a teenager must be:

- realistic.

You are not perfect as a parent (sorry!) and it is totally unrealistic to expect that your adolescent will be perfect.

- enforceable.

Don't threaten a teenager if you're not prepared to back up your threat. 'Don't ever darken my door again if you carry on seeing that boy/girl' can have truly disastrous consequences.

- beneficial for the family.

Explain why boundaries are in place – the eleven o'clock curfew is there because other family members have to sleep, there's school in the morning and so on. Negotiate with your teenager and make them feel heard, but do be prepared to stand your ground.

So, part of the internal change for adolescents is the need to make a huge number of decisions that may have very important consequences. What other things does an adolescent need to have in their psychological armoury?

Who are you?

Ah, yes . . . if this wasn't confusing enough already, let's throw in one of the fundamentals of philosophy! We said earlier that people have an internal world as well as an external one. Now we know that a big part of this internal world is the ability to make decisions in the external world. We know that such decisions are difficult to make for adolescents because they lack an experience base and are making many important calls for the first time. Another reason why these choices are difficult is because adolescents lack a stable sense of self; to some extent, as with clothes and fashions, adolescents try on personalities to see which is the best fit. Let me explain in a bit more depth.

At my venerable age (thirty-two again), I know a lot of the things that I like and I know there are things I don't like. I can give a description of what I am like as a person who has been relatively stable for a period of years (please note the use of the word 'relatively'). My friends would describe certain behaviours as being 'out of character' or 'not like him at all' if I were to do them, implying that there is a relatively stable character and a 'him' who I am like. When I make a decision, even if its an absolute disaster (which is often the case; mistakes are not the sole province of adolescents), there is a 'me' to fall back on, who has certain experiences, certain attributes and certain qualities and along with it, a sense that 'I'll be OK.'

Adolescents don't yet have this relatively stable sense of self. If you remember Harry Enfield's classic and superbly observed character, 'Kevin the Teenager', one of the amusing things about him was that he behaved in one way with his parents – dismissive, frustrated, and contemptuous – and in another way with his friend's parents – respectful, polite, subordinate. This is because Kevin was finding his way and working out day by day what type of person he was, based on all manner of different expectations, beliefs and ways of constructing the world.

Parents often say about their adolescents things like 'Oh, he/she was such a lovely little boy/girl, never caused me any trouble. Now look at them!'

We know that adolescents struggle with all the huge physical changes that they go through but the enormous psychological changes that occur to their sense of who they are, are no less confusing – indeed, sometimes they are significantly worse. It's easy to look around and spot that other adolescents of your age and sex are sprouting breasts or underarm hair; it's another thing entirely to know that all other adolescents are also going through periods of agonising self doubt, confusion and feeling lost.

So how on earth can a poor adolescent develop a sense of self upon which to build his decisions? The answer is through two processes known as separation and individuation.

These two processes are really intertwined, but as you've probably guessed by now, psychologists love to complicate things.

Separation and individuation

It is very difficult for parents to accept that their children are growing up. This is partly because just as parents have got their heads around being a parent and are beginning to feel like they know what they're doing, their child changes out of all recognition. It's also due to the fact that having been the be-all and end-all of their children's lives for so long, suddenly parents are supplanted by other spotty adolescents, Eminem and various teenage magazines; parents are frightened that they are losing control of their child who is making decisions that they are hopelessly ill-equipped to make, ready for entry into an adult world that they seem far too young to be entering.

As a child develops into a teenager, their social 'web' becomes more important. The opinions of their peers become a matter of life and death and the need for acceptance becomes critical. Gangs form, cliques form. What is utterly, obviously, clearly 'in' today, is totally, completely and hopelessly 'out' tomorrow, depending on who is saying what. In other words, a teenager is separating from their parents' world and influence and going through the process of individuation – becoming a unique individual with ideas of their own. Incidentally, this is why many adolescents hate being referred to as 'Mr Jones's little boy,' or 'Steven's little sister' – adolescence is hard enough without people constantly identifying you as an extension of someone else!

For adolescents, establishing their own identity is hard.

The processes separation and individuation are both necessary and difficult for parents. Parents can resist separation as much as their adolescents and remember that this process is not just the physical separation that occurs when, for example, a child leaves for university, but the psychological separation that occurs when children become distinct from their parents. Some parents find this a terrible prospect and do whatever they can to cling to their offspring, treating their decisions and opinions with some degree of contempt and undermining their attempts to grow up. The process of individuation is equally problematic. Imagine parents who adopt the view that only their opinions matter and who dominate their teenager – imagine how ill-prepared that teenager will be for the adult world.

For the teenager, these processes are the bedrock for their development into adults. It's difficult to be an adult if all your opinions and ideas are exactly the same as your parents or if you meekly follow the behaviours of your peers. What is important for adolescents is that they are able to internalise a model, not only of their own identity, but also the identity of their parents. This is going back to something that we mentioned a long time ago in Chapter 1, the idea of a secure base from which to explore the world.

If adolescents believe that their parents will be there for them no matter what they do, it is easier for them to go out and explore, make mistakes and learn their own way. If adolescents don't believe this, then they risk trying to grow up too soon and getting lost, or they become so anxious that they refuse to take any decisions themselvesand thus delay entry into adulthood by deferring constantly to others.

Just to sum up some of what we've been talking about so far in this chapter.

The main psychological goal of adolescence is creating an identity that is separate and distinct from those around you.

This is achieved through the twin processes of individuation and separation.

As these lengthy processes go on, an individual becomes more able to make balanced decisions and have more realistic goals since their decisions are based on a more secure internal model of themselves and those around them.

During these processes, adolescents will boundary-test to try and work out what is and isn't acceptable for them. Parents have to learn what are and are not acceptable boundaries and whereas the first ten years of a child's life are often described as a juggling act for parents, the next are sometimes described as a tightrope act, finding and adapting balances for the family, while taking into consideration the fact that adolescents are often out of balance.

Emotional regulation

So now we know a bit about some of the psychological processes that adolescents go through. Something else that adolescents must master – and remember that this is all going on in a context of increasing physical, social and educational strain – is how to regulate their emotions.

We know that adolescents are prone to hormone tempests and that these hormones are partly responsible for the changes in emotion that adolescents suffer. The increasing demands that are placed on adolescents mean that they have more to react to, and the emotional outbursts that are so common in adolescence are often a consequence of the demands on the teenager exceeding their perceived ability to cope.

Moods in adolescents tend to be longer lasting than in children: whereas a child may sulk for a few hours, a bad mood in a teenager can last for days. They also tend to be more intense. Adolescents can feel on top of the world, as if they are floating on air, because so-and-so said 'yes' to a date at the pictures and in a never-ending inferno of misery because they then changed their mind and said 'no'. Embarrassment at a perceived faux pas can go on for weeks, disappointments are seen as eternal and, as parents will no doubt be sick of hearing:

'You, Mum and Dad, just don't understand!'

Why are these emotions so intense? Well, for a similar reason to the question about why it's difficult for adolescents to make decisions – some of these emotions are being experienced for the first time. Many adults still remember their first broken heart, their first kiss, their first major disappointment thirty or forty years after the event. Why? Because they are so profoundly memorable. They leave a real emotional mark on us. For the teenager experiencing these things today, they can be revolutionary and extremely hard to bear.

Adolescents learn through experience that these emotions are not crippling or unendurable. They learn that emotions come and go and they learn techniques for handling them. But while they are experiencing them, there are a few things that parents can do to make the ride a little less bumpy.

• Remember how it was for you.

You have more life experience than your teenager – use it! Parents can really forge bonds with their adolescents by admitting that the same things happened to them, explaining what they did to get over them and how they survived. The advice can be offered, rather than forced on them; adolescents need to experience for themselves the fact that their emotions won't kill them.

• Give them space . . .

'Are you sure you're all right, dear?' asked for the fifteenth time, while well meaning, can also be wildly infuriating. It can be far better for parents to simply say, 'That must be really difficult, I'm sorry things are rough. If you need a chat, I'm available.'

• . . . but remember the boundaries.

Adolescents must learn that rampaging emotions are not a valid excuse for misdemeanours. Just as an adult must appreciate that saying 'Well, I just lost my rag and hit someone/got drunk and drove into a lamppost' avoids responsibility and is an explanation, not a valid excuse, so must adolescents learn that their anger and frustration are not just cause for hurting or upsetting someone else. The boundaries that have been put in place can be loosened temporarily, but can't be allowed to fall out of use altogether – there are other people living in the house as well. We all have to learn that no matter what is going on for us, life has to go on.

- Don't lose your head.

Now I can see a lot of parents out there sneering at this one. I know it's one thing to say it and another to do it when your teenager is standing there screaming 'What do you know about it?' If you are drawn into confrontation with your teenager, perhaps because he or she is lashing out emotionally, remember that this is an opportunity to model how emotions can be dealt with – rationally, calmly and without the need for all-out warfare or revenge.

Take it easy when talking to a teenager; make your point, say what you have to say and leave it at that.

Now you know your teenager inside and out! The internal changes during adolescence could fill another book (must send a note to my editor!) but I hope that this has given you a taste of how complex the teenage years are in terms of psychological development; perhaps it even stirs the odd memory or two of how complicated it was for you.

INFORMATION POINT 3

Moral development

We now know a little bit about the changes in adolescents both physically and psychologically. One area in which there are profound changes is the often-neglected area of moral development and knowing what is right and wrong. Younger children's morals are often based upon avoiding punishment and simply getting their needs met. But many psychologists, like Jean Piaget and

Lawrence Kohlberg, feel that other levels of moral development occur as a child grows. In adolescence, the important areas seem to be operating according to the expectations of others and according to social norms but also developing a personal morality which may or may not be the same as the norms of society. For example, the adolescent who smokes cannabis may be doing it to rebel, but they may also be doing it because they see no moral reason not to; as they develop their own moral code, they may find themselves at loggerheads with the morals of their parents. Is it morally acceptable for a person to protest against a perceived government injustice, even if it's on an illegal march? It's a fascinating area that has been under-researched, but parents are very lucky in this respect: they get to observe the development of a moral code in their children.

As we know by now, adolescents don't live in a vacuum. There's a whole big wide world out there that they have to deal with. In the next chapter, we'll look at the adolescent's social world and the pressures that they have to face and we'll also look at some of the hot questions of the day, namely the role of violent movies and video games, music and all sorts of other goodies. See you there!

> Premature burial works just fine
> as a cure for adolescence.
>
> (George Alec Effinger, author)

Chapter 4   Who's afraid of the evil dead?

The young always have the same problem –
how to rebel and conform at the same time. They have
now solved this by defying their parents
and copying one another.
(Quentin Crisp, author and actor)

External pressures

In this chapter, we're going to look at some of the external pressures that the adolescent – full of hormones, changing physically, confused internally and desperately trying to make sense of it all – have to endure.

Parents often say that they are confused by some of the things they see, hear and read in the media and are often very concerned about the impact that certain things, whether it be Eminem's latest CD (for 'Eminem' read 'artist that swears a lot') or the latest horror or sexually graphic movie or video game, are going to have on their teenager. We'll start with a little potted history of pop culture and its influence on adolescents.

To begin . . . a little history

In the fifties, around the time that 'Cool' was born, the millennia-old battle between parents and their teenage offspring took on a new dimension. Adolescents were at risk of becoming 'JDs' – juvenile delinquents – epitomised by the late, great JD himself, James Dean.

JDs drank too much, smoked too much, drove too fast and wore strange clothes. There was Elvis, with his hip-swinging invtations to sexuality, cutting a swath through parental notions of what constituted 'a good tune' and Marlon Brando redefining youth's quest for identity – 'What are you rebelling against?' 'What have you got?'

Parents panicked that their adolescents were growing up too fast and the media issued dire warnings about the influence of 'jungle rhythms' and a loss of morality.

When the decade changed, so did the points of conflict between families. Drugs, the terrible 'reefer madness' caused by smoking cannabis now threatened Western youth, as did the music of the times – the wild antics of the Who, the establishment battles against the Rolling Stones, and of course, those crazy mop-tops, the Beatles.

In the seventies, youth culture in England produced the Sex Pistols and their rallying cry 'No Future'. Parents looked on aghast as their teenage children went out (in public!) wearing fishnets and nose rings.

In the eighties, fashions seemed to change too quickly to even keep track, from New Romantics through to House, whilst the nineties brought with them ecstasy – another 'evil drug menace'.

Now we find ourselves in the new millennium and surprisingly enough, nothing much has changed. The media delights in drawing attention to activities or issues with headlines such as 'Ban This Evil Filth' or a variant thereof. There is always an artist or artists who create something that flies in the face of some social norms. (Although stick around long enough and they usually go 'mainstream' – anyone been shocked by Madonna recently? Marilyn Manson? Nope.)

The reason always given by the media for drawing attention to these so-called 'outrages' is the need to 'protect our children' and of course has nothing to do with the need to sell more papers or make you watch this particular TV programme – isn't it nice to know your media are so altruistic?

Those of us who are old enough or cynical enough (or both in my case) realise that, although the names may change, the fears and worries that the media prey upon over the years are pretty much the same.

But it's important to remember that adolescents are coming into contact with these things for the first time. For example: the fears that were whipped up around marijuana in the fifties (that the drug would lead to instant madness and addiction and inevitable death) are very similar to those whipped up around ecstasy, obscuring the facts about both.

Because it can be hard for adolescents to feel their way into having a clear-cut identity for themselves, it's easy for them to strongly identify with external things, like movie stars, pop stars and so on, even to the extent of mimicking their mannerisms, speech patterns and dress.

This process of identification (combined with the processes we looked at in the last chapter) is part of growing up. Add to the mix the peer group and we have a vitally important recipe for emotional, social and psychological development. Now let's take a closer look at the peer group and some of the pros and cons that can arise from it.

Peers and peer pressure

No man is an island, as the old cliché goes, and perhaps it is never truer than during adolescence. Come on, parents – you must remember those lonely Friday nights where you were sure everyone else apart from you was out having a great time and you felt as if you were never going to have the boyfriend/girlfriend that you were sure everyone else had – or was that just me?

For adolescents, who are feeling very unsure of themselves as they struggle to deal with all sorts of different pressures and changes like the ones we've looked at, having friends of the same age and with the same interests is critical.

How peers help

Peers are very important in assisting with the processes of separation and individuation that we looked at in Chapter 3 because:

- Peers act as a mirror.

An adolescent's peer group provides reinforcement of their growing identity. Adolescents discover, through their peers, that their likes, interests and ideas are shared. Furthermore, this shows them that these things have value and by extension, that they themselves have value as people.

- Peers act as a testing ground.

Adolescents can test out ideas, jokes, behaviours and so on with their peers that they wouldn't feel comfortable doing with their parents – or, indeed, that wouldn't be appropriate to do with their parents. Just as a family develops its own 'story' that has morals, codes, things that are OK and things that aren't, so too does the peer group.

• **Peers provide social support and safety.**

'First times' are more fun celebrated with a group than on your own. It might be that first illicit cigarette, getting into the cinema underage, that first can of beer – the peer group provides the opportunity for an adolescent to celebrate new things and new experiences and commiserate first disasters.

• **Peers don't live in the same house.**

As we have seen, adolescents are starting to separate from their family and sometimes, even in the most harmonious of households, the peer group acts as an escape valve from the stresses and strains of family life. Also, it is something separate and private from the family that the adolescent has built up by him/herself. It is therefore precious and important and criticism of the peer group can be a big mistake as it suggests that the adolescent hasn't got the ability to create things for themselves away from the family.

Peer pressure

Unfortunately, it is one of the ironies of adolescence that in the drive to separate and individuate from the family, there is often enormous pressure on a young person to conform from what are often fragile peer groups.

Peer groups can be very difficult places to be; there is jostling for position as 'top dog' in male groups, often marked by fights; fighting also exists in female groups, but there is often more emotional pressure exerted on its members; and there is often competition between the two groups as boys and girls start to become attracted to the opposite sex as potential partners. In other words, there is 'peer pressure'.

If a peer group identifies itself in certain ways – perhaps according to musical tastes, or movies or sporting activities – then, by definition, it is not other things.

For example, the captain of the girls' hockey team may have as a peer group other hockey players. Hockey players may look down with contempt on 'the swots' or the intellectual students. There maybe pressure on an intellectual hockey player to leave the studying to others, causing a dip in their academic performance.

Peer pressure exerts itself in other ways, too. A drive to experiment and test out new abilities is a normal part of growing up. If the 'gang' has decided that this weekend's homework will be to find out what happens if we drink ten pints of beer, this may come too soon for some and they may resist the pressure from their peers.

However, if the cost of resisting this pressure is exclusion from the newly created 'gang' and being labelled as a 'chicken' or a 'coward', then the pressure to conform and take part anyway may well be greater. Bowing to peer pressure can cause enormous stress and self-doubt.

There can be a pressure to do everything all at once and sometimes this is simply too soon; some people are genuinely ready to try sex at the age of sixteen, others really aren't. Experimentation with drugs and also with petty crime are not uncommon and, again, there can be enormous pressure to try these things before a person is either prepared for them or even sure about whether they want to try them at all.

What is difficult for parents is the knowledge that their adolescent is becoming part of a growing world that they are simply not involved in and probably don't want to be involved in. Parents are really walking something of a tightrope, as we mentioned before: get too involved with your adolescent's world and you are at risk of them kicking against you and trying to exclude you or, perhaps even worse, failing to separate from you; on the other hand, if you are too laissez faire, your adolescent may try more and more extreme ways of getting you to set boundaries for them.

How to deal with a peer group

> Teenagers complain there's nothing to do, then stay out all night doing it.
>
> (Bob Phillips, author)

Here are a few suggestions that may help you when it comes to dealing with your teenager's peer group:

• Offer your services.

Being the taxi service for your teenager and their friends can be a great way of getting to know them. Being a host also means that whatever is going on, is going on under your roof and adolescents are less likely to push their luck if they identify you along the lines of 'Your dad seems all right' rather than 'Your dad's a right so and so, isn't he?'

Dad's taxi!

- Be interested.

Once you know the people who are in your adolescent's peer groups, ask about them, show interest, just as you would do in your friends' social groups. Don't be too intrusive, don't be pushy. Your adolescent son or daughter wants to be treated like an adult and this is a perfect opportunity.

- Don't label or judge.

It is a fairly safe bet that there will be people in your adolescent's social group who you don't like. This does not necessarily mean that they are evil. If you have a partner, there are probably people in their social group who you don't like, and, if you have in-laws, that probability may become a near-certainty. We make mistakes in our choices of friends and we learn to deal with them.

- 'They're leading my little baby astray.'

The worries and fears that parents have about their adolescents can combine in this one phrase. There is a very real fear that adolescents will go down a path that is irreversible; that the peer group will supplant the parents and that the parents will become irrelevant; and there can be a profound sense of loss now that their children are growing up and may soon be fleeing the nest. These fears are often not grounded in reality, but the presence of a peer group can serve to amplify them.

In this case, what becomes important is a sense of trust. It becomes necessary to trust, firstly, that you have done the best job that you could have done and that you have prepared your children for the big wide world.

Secondly, it becomes necessary to trust that your children are beginning to be able to make good decisions and develop instincts that will serve them well; and thirdly, to trust that whatever scrapes your adolescent gets into, they will always have you to turn to.

Educational strain

The educational system places a huge strain on students. Academic workload goes up for anyone preparing for GCSEs and 'A' levels. The pressure can be very great and it's thrown into the mix with all the other pressures that adolescents go through, creating something that can be called 'role strain': literally the stress caused by having to play certain roles, some of which are very difficult.

An adolescent having to play the roles of student, son/daughter, and brother/sister is nearly but not quite an adult, has a role or position to play in their peer group and is also quite probably having their first relationships with members of the opposite sex. Having to get your homework in on time can really be the last straw.

Adolescents often lament that schoolwork is a waste of time or pointless and sometimes they are quite right. Adolescents don't yet have the 'long-term' view that adults develop and so if it's a choice between getting an essay done on German chancellors during the nineteenth century or going to what promises to be the greatest party of all time, it can be pretty difficult to see the plus side of spending three hours in the library.

However, homework and exams are part of the growing number of responsibilities that adolescents have to face. Getting homework done can be tied into the negotiation that goes on within families, for example, 'Yes, you can go to the party, *if* you get your homework done.'

Homework and exams are
a growing responsibility for adolescents.

It is an important lesson to learn that life is not always fun – there are sometimes things that we have to do in order to get to enjoy the things that we want to do. Academic qualifications can be seen as hoops that have to be jumped through in order to move on to other things.

If you can help your teenager with their schoolwork then by all means do so; be understanding of the stresses that they are under, especially at exam time; and if extra help is needed, talk to the school and see what can be organised.

Again, there is another balance to be struck. Success as a human being shouldn't be measured by success in exams, but they do have their function.

Organising some careers advice can be helpful, because it puts the exams in some sort of context: 'If I get these results then I can do this.'

Are violent video games, violent movies, Internet sites and/or explicit lyrics in music bad for people?

This topic has caused a lot of controversy in the last twenty-five years or so. The film, *The Evil Dead*,

85

could be regarded as the start of it all – the moral panic, the worry that watching the film might turn you into some kind of addled lunatic. (Hence, the title of this chapter – it wasn't a reference to what teenagers look like in the mornings!)

Video games are a new slant – a recent newspaper article found that 'sexually explicit' downloads for games could be found on the Internet, including one that made Lara Croft slightly more interesting than usual.

Furthermore, there has been concern about the content of some Internet sites and the sexual exploitation of children via 'chat rooms' that are difficult to monitor.

The bottom line on all of this seems to be:

- Letting children watch TV or play video games for five or more hours a day is bad for them if they are not doing anything else.

There has been an explosion of obesity and weight

problems in children and adolescents and lack of activity combined with bad diet are two major factors. Furthermore, this is a key stage for the development of social skills and these are not going to develop if your only interaction is with a TV set.

Again, negotiate with your adolescents if they're hogging the TV to play on their PlayStation. If they have a TV in their room, ask them what they're playing or watching and join in.

- These things are more likely to be problematic if they occur out of context.

If parents do not listen to music or watch movies then they are not in a position to judge if they are bad or not, nor are they in a position to put these experiences in context. Parents can take the shock value out of things by *not* being shocked and horrified and immediately writing to the newspaper, but rather by talking about these things with their children.

87

- Exposure to violent material does not necessarily cause violent behaviour.

If it did, then anyone who watched the news on TV would be in deep trouble. What adolescents do need to have is a critical framework within which to judge such things. Parents can help with simple comments like 'You know you can't do that stuff in real life, don't you?' or 'Do you think younger kids should watch this stuff?'

Do remember that responding to your teenager's actions (or choices) with parental hysteria is a sure-fire way to ensure that the behaviour will continue.

If you make something sound dangerous and edgy or lay down the law along the lines of 'Not in this house, you don't' then adolescents will be attracted to it. Be low key about this kind of thing, joke about it and remember that the Sex Pistols would have been a lot less shocking if people hadn't been shocked by them.

Adolescent males will 'read' top-shelf magazines and probably watch pornographic movies, too. This is finding out about sex within a peer group and is not, in itself, harmful and finding a copy of a top-shelf magazine under the bed is not evidence of perversion!

Internet sites can be monitored and certain content blocked. Chat rooms are, again, not in and of themselves dangerous, but meeting people through chat rooms should be discussed thoroughly with adolescents: sixteen-year-old Catherine may well turn out to be sixty-year-old Charlie. Discuss this with your son or daughter and use common sense.

INFORMATION POINT 4

When disaster strikes

Everybody makes mistakes. Mistakes are valuable learning experiences but they can also be very painful. Sometimes, the mistakes are big ones.

It's very common for adolescents, in their drive to discover themselves, to find things in their own personality that aren't pleasant and to find themselves making mistakes that do have serious consequences, whether that be unprotected sex, involvement with the police, problems at school, problems on the road after passing a driving test, drinking too much or dabbling with drugs.

Teenage drinking and driving can have
serious consequences.

It's important for all parties:

- to remain calm.

Even when the temptation for the adolescent is to run away and for the parents to pack their bags for them.

- to get the facts straight.

It's important for everybody to know exactly what happened so that the appropriate course of action can be taken.

- not to make things worse by fighting about it.

There are times to say 'I told you so' and 'How could you be so dumb?' This is almost certainly not one of them.

An adolescent will know that they have messed up, even though they may try to pretend that it's nothing. A lecture can wait. This is a time for considered action, rather than hasty accusations.

What family members can expect from each other

In this chapter, we've looked at some of the social pressures that adolescents have to cope with. In the next, we'll come full circle and take a closer look at the family – however it is constructed – and look at what family members can expect from each other.

As you might have guessed, what family members want from each other are often not the same things!

Chapter 5   *Parenting advice*

> Having a child no more makes you a parent than
> having a piano makes you a pianist.
> (Michael Levine, American author)

Parenting your teenage offspring

I hope you've caught your breath from the first four chapters, because in this one I'm going to throw lots of ideas and hints at you about parenting your teenage offspring.

This book is about adolescents, rather than families but as we all know by now (all together!) 'adolescents don't live in a vacuum'. They live in a changing physical world and carry on their lives as their personalities and internal worlds change, all the time being influenced by their peers. They also usually live in a family – a unit that is also changing all the time.

Entire books are written on the ways that families function and how to fine tune parenting styles (I do hope my editor is picking up these hints!) but in this

93

chapter we'll focus on some examples of parental responses to their adolescents and the pros and the cons of each.

Please remember: don't worry if you're not doing all the things that are suggested all the time. No parent is perfect and it's one thing to see the examples set down on paper, quite another to be doing them while juggling a relationship, a job, other children and all that living stuff that goes on in between.

> Let your children be the teenager he or she
> wants to be, not the adolescent you were
> or wish you had been.
> (Laurence Steinberg, psychologist)

DR DAVE'S SUPER-FAST PARENTING QUIZ

To start us off, let me invite you to take part in the quiz that follows. It's just like me – short and simple – so don't take too long over your answers and no dictionaries, calculators or cheating!

Just pick the answer that suits you best!

1. You find your fourteen-year-old son smoking out of the bedroom window.

You had previously told him that you didn't want him smoking in the house.

What do you say?

a. 'I told you I didn't want you smoking in the house. If you must do it – and you know what I think about it – do it outside.'

b. 'Oh, well, we've all got our vices. Got a fag for your Mum?'

c. 'I *bleep* told you what would happen if you *bleep* smoked in the house!'

2. Your fourteen-year-old daughter wants her new seventeen-year-old boyfriend to stay the night. You think she's been influenced by her nineteen-year-old sister who has a boyfriend at university.

You reply:

a. 'Now we've talked about this before. It's one thing for your sister to stay with her boyfriend, but this is different. We all want to get to know him a bit better.'

b. 'Oh, well, if your sister's doing it, I suppose you feel left out. Just this once, mind. I'll make the bed up.'

c. 'Are you crazy? It's illegal for one thing! I knew that crazy sister of yours was a bad influence!'

3. Your fifteen-year-old son is struggling at school and announces he's just going to stop going .

How do you respond?

a. 'I know it's really difficult at the moment. But you've got to keep going until you finish the year. Then we can look at your options.'

b. 'Why don't you turn up for the classes that you like and skip the others?'

c. 'No son of mine is going to be a drop out! Get back to work!'

4. You get the dreaded phone call from school asking you to come in and meet with a teacher. Your thirteen-year-old daughter has been accused of bullying.

What do you say when she comes in from school?

a. 'We've had a phone call from school to go to a meeting about bullying. I'd like to hear your side of it first.'

b. 'Guess that snotty-nosed twerp was asking for it, eh?'

c. 'Accused of bullying? Do you have any idea how embarrassing this is for us all? What were you thinking?'

5. You've found what appears to be some drug paraphernalia in your daughter's bedroom. You're extremely worried and unsure what to do about it.

What do you say to her?

a. 'Listen, I need a word with you. I was cleaning your room today and I found some things lying about that I don't understand. Can you explain them to me?'

b. Nothing – children have to make their own way in the world.

c. 'I don't know what the hell this stuff is, but I'm warning you, I find anything like this again, and it's the police I'll be calling.'

6. Your seventeen-year-old son has been looking increasingly miserable over the last few months and has been angry and snappy. He announces one day that he wants to leave home and if you disagree then he'll run away.

    You say:

    a. 'Well, that doesn't give us a lot of room to manoeuvre, does it? What do you want us to do? How can we help?'

    b. 'Well, we can't let you run away. We'll look for somewhere for you to go and stay tomorrow, shall we?'

    c. 'Think it's that easy, do you? Running away from your responsibilities? How'd you like it if I ran away from my responsibilities and stopped paying the bills?'

There are no points awarded on this quiz, but it does illustrate some different types of parental response to tricky situations.

Let's have a look at the pros and cons inherent in each of them.

The 'C' response

Starting with the last response, the 'C' response could be described as the immediate, no-stopping-to-think response. It's the one where emotion is primary, rather than thought.

In the first question, the one about smoking, this angry 'How dare you' response is probably going through many parents' minds. It's a straightforward answer, blunt and clear.

However, it also reinforces the idea of power – what the parent says, goes. The problem with this is that many adolescents are questioning the idea of parental control very strongly and such a parental response invites an aggressive comeback. This type of response risks escalation – an attempted solution to the problem becomes a problem itself and a row may ensue between the parent and the adolescent that has nothing whatsoever to do with the initial problem.

The 'C' response highlights some other problems raised by this type of emotional response.

Firstly, it tends to bring the issue round to how the parent is feeling at the time ('Don't you realise how embarrassing this is for us?'/'How'd you like it if I ran away from my responsibilities?') instead of dealing with the problem.

Secondly, what the adolescent is likely to pick up from this sort of response is that Mum and Dad are 'always blowing things out of proportion/ always yelling. Why can't they just chill out?'

Thirdly, always being in a state of emotional explosion is an extremely stressful standpoint for parents to take. Going immediately to DefCon 5 also means that there is nowhere for the parent to go. If children say to themselves 'Wow, I hope Mum and Dad aren't angry about this' then clearly, Mum and Dad getting angry is still a deterrent. If instead they simply think 'There he goes, blowing his top again' then this is no deterrent at all, which really defeats the purpose.

Many people remember the teacher at school who never seemed to scream or shout but who always maintained order and respect while the ones who always had the volume turned up to eleven were often regarded with contempt.

In other words:

- Focus on the problem and on the adolescent, not yourself.

- Model calm, rational responses.

- Don't give yourself an ulcer because your child had a puff on a cigarette. If that's the worst they do while they're growing up, then you're doing pretty well.

- Parental anger should be a deterrent not an everyday occurrence, otherwise it loses its force.

INFORMATION POINT 5
Physical force against children

It should be noted at this point that some parents believe that physical force is a valid way to get their children to do what they want. With high rates of domestic violence in the UK and a high incidence of violence against children, there has been a sea change in this country.

Although UK law still accepts the principle of 'reasonable chastisement' (an idea dating back to 1860!), there are more and more moves to protect children from harm and to see that children and adolescents have the same rights as adults.

There is also more and more research evidence to suggest that:

- Physical violence against children, even what some might mistakenly describe as 'mild' physical punishment, causes physical and psychological damage.

- Using physical chastisement against children and adolescents is ineffective – although it may cause a behaviour to stop in the short term (probably due to shock and pain) it is ineffective in the long term.

- Physical chastisement damages relationships between family members.

Just as physical violence between adults is no way to resolve anything, so physical violence from a parent to a child (of whatever age) is no longer acceptable. Several countries in Europe have already banned smacking and it seems that the UK is also moving in this direction.

If as a parent, you are losing your cool to the point where you think you may lash out, leave the situation. Walk away. Go and calm down. Hitting a child – of whatever age – could cause you to lose far more than your temper.

The 'B' response

The 'B' response is in some ways the opposite of the 'C' response. Often good ideas underpin the 'B' response, such as:

- Kids have to find their own way in the world and make mistakes.

- I want to be a friend to my kids.

- I don't want my child to feel excluded from family activities.

- I must support my child at all times.

These are good ideas, but often in practice, they go a little bit haywire. Children do have to find their own way and make mistakes. But what they also need is a framework within which to make mistakes. William Golding's classic book *The Lord of the Flies* shows what can happen when children try to make their own rules; lacking a framework of compassion for others, responsibility and so on, the rules are often simply based on 'looking after number one'.

If the results of their actions are not set out for them, adolescents avoid learning an important lesson: their behaviours have consequences. This can be disastrous for their development.

It's a great thing to want to be a friend to your children. But perhaps what is more important is to be what they want you to be. Adolescents are making their own friends, developing their own peer group, which is confusing enough. They need a boundary drawn between these friends and their parents.

Although it's no bad thing for parents and children to do things together, having a parent who is also a friend can be highly confusing. Be friendly, sure, but that boundary must be drawn. Friends often talk about their personal problems, difficulties, and so on. But a parent's problems are their own and adolescents need to be able to feel that their parents can deal with their own problems. Otherwise, the risk is that adolescents are drawn into an adult world before they are ready.

Not wanting your children to feel excluded is also a good thing, but there are times when it's inevitable. If you're having a heart-to-heart talk with your seventeen-year-old daughter about the boyfriend who slept with her and then dumped her, it's very unlikely she'd want her ten-year-old brother listening in. Your seventeen-year-old daughter may still be a teenager, but broken hearts and emotional pain are adult stuff and it's not appropriate to involve younger children in such discussions. Perhaps the ten-year-old brother could be told that his sister is 'having a bit of a hard time at the moment' and leave it at that.

The desire to support a child at all times is an admirable one, but sometimes an impossible one to put into practice. If your eleven-year-old decides they want to run away and join the circus, it might be a more appropriate idea to buy them a set of juggling balls rather than giving them the airfare to go join the Moscow State Circus. Even though parents have to learn how to give some responsibility to their adolescents, giving them too much responsibility before they are ready can be just as damaging as giving them none. Now let's have a look at the 'A' response.

The 'A' response

What can a parent learn from the 'A' response? In the replies to the questions about smoking and the boyfriend coming to stay, they offer consistency.

'If you must smoke – do it outside!'

They refer back to previous discussions and simply restate the position that has already been offered. It's important to note that these positions can and should change dependent on the circumstances; if our fourteen-year-old is being told that when she's twenty-four she can't have her boyfriend of ten years to stay in the same room, it's likely that she will come to regard her folks, at best, as somewhat behind the times, at worst, as lunatics!

However, much as adolescents may protest, consistency is vital for them to be able to learn to predict how the world works. Inconsistent parents (that is, parents that wilt and change their minds over things under pressure or mums and dads that can't agree on a position together) can cause huge confusion for adolescents at a difficult time in their development. Consistency provides boundaries and allows an adolescent to know where they stand. If Dad says 'A' and Mum says 'B' then their children will drive a bus through this position and attempts at enforcing boundaries will become impossible.

The 'A' answers are also explanatory and cooperative. They explain the motivation behind why things are as they are. No parent can offer perfect explanations all of the time; even though all parents promise themselves that they will never say 'Because I say so!' to their children, it does happen from time to time and can be helpful if it's in the context of usually providing explanations for things. Adolescents begin to learn the art of being able to explain why they are doing things.

Cooperation in family matters is essential. Just as outside in the real world, egos have to be checked in at the door sometimes. We can't have it all our own way and believe me, I've tried!

Cooperation and its sibling, compromise, are skills that are learnt as we go through life and they go towards developing a repertoire of assertive skills. Assertive adolescents are the ones who are skilled not only at cooperating with others in order to achieve mutually beneficial ends but also at compromising and acknowledging that they can't have it all their own way.

This is in stark contrast to aggressive adolescents

(my way or the highway/no compromise) and passive adolescents (your way is better than mine/my opinions do not have value).

Furthermore, the cooperative answer seen in the 'A' response to question three (the one about wanting to leave school) shows the teenager that they are not alone and that some of the burden they are facing can be shared, whilst at the same time indicating that they have to do a lot of the work – it's their life after all.

The last three 'A' answers (to questions four, five and six) give examples of useful skills:

• They keep the lines of communication open.

The blunderbuss approach of the 'C' response slams the door of conversation shut and invites a row, whereas the more conciliatory approach of the 'A' response means that even if the teenager needs to hide away in their cave for a bit, there is always an opportunity for talk and discussion.

- They keep things low key.

We already know that some of the decisions that adolescents make are not ones that their parents approve of. However, this needs to be accepted by parents and a low-key response given when the occasion arises. There really is no need to make the situation worse.

- They invite adult responses by being adult.

Adult responses from adolescents do not usually come out of nowhere. They are often modelled on adult responses from others. If an adolescent is shown by their parents that things can be dealt with calmly and rationally they are more likely to adopt this position themselves, especially if they see how such calm responses are more likely to lead to a positive outcome.

More top tips for a harmonious home

Family contracts

There often has to be a division of labour in a

family when household tasks have to be divided up among family members. A good way to diffuse potential trouble spots is to draw up a contract in the form of a timetable for the week so that every one knows who is doing what and when: Monday, it's Mum's turn to take the rubbish out; Tuesday, it's seventeen-year-old John's turn to clean the kitchen; Wednesday, it's fourteen-year-old Katie's turn to take the dog for a walk; and so on.

'Who's walking the dog?'

The family can also agree on what happens if these things aren't done: perhaps it's three days straight of walking the dog. The point is that rather than having 'it's-your-turn-no-it's-yours' arguments, a resolute finger can simply be pointed at the timetable stuck on the fridge. It can be particularly helpful in busy families, where first dibs have to be put on the car!

Don't make your timetable a hyper-complicated, colour-coded, 3-D thing; make it fun. Creating a family contract is a good example of everybody sitting around the table and getting a problem sorted out and good way of showing adolescents that everybody is in the same boat.

Not in front of the kids

We have looked at a range of things that parents can do for their adolescent offspring in terms of the responses that they offer to their children.

One thing that is often forgotten is parental behaviour and it's absolutely critical. There is a wealth of literature surrounding the negative impact on adolescents of parental behaviour such as shouting, fighting, arguments and drunkenness. Such behaviour definitely does affect the behaviour of children, but parents often forget this in the heat of the moment.

Justifications, such as 'Seeing her Mum and Dad arguing, teaches her how to hold her own in an argument', are rubbish; they assume that a teenager sees the situation from the same point of view as their parents, which they don't. What a child sees in this situation is the parents trying to pull themselves apart, which leads to insecurity and anxiety. Rows do occur in families, but they shouldn't be allowed to take precedence over the wellbeing of the children. Please, take a deep breath and have the conversation later.

Drunkenness and fighting from parents show children that their parents are out of control, which is a very scary place to be for a child of whatever age. It also models behaviour that may be highly inappropriate: thirteen-year-olds getting drunk or unable to resolve conflict without the use of their fists have modelled their behaviour on that of their parents with wide-ranging and often disastrous consequences.

Stuck record technique

A technique that many parents find helpful when discussing things with their children is the 'stuck record' technique. It can often be the case in conflicts, that the actual point of the discussion gets lost in the heated argument. The stuck record technique is really a way of keeping 'on-message' and avoiding the debate getting too emotionally charged.

For example:

Daughter: Dad, can I borrow the car tonight to go and see Paul?

Dad: Sorry, hon, you know I need it tonight.

Daughter: But it's really, really important that I use the car!

Dad: I'm sorry, but you know I need the car every Tuesday night.

Daughter: Couldn't you just let me have it this once? It's really important!

Dad: Sorry, it's Tuesday and I need it.

Daughter: That's just typical! You just won't see how important this is for me, will you? You're so selfish!

Dad: Yep, I am selfish, it is still Tuesday and I need the car.

Now Dad has to use this technique with care – if he knows for example, that he doesn't really need the car and he's just being mean then this technique has been misused. If, on the other hand, he has made it perfectly clear that on Tuesdays the car is off limits then this technique can be helpful. It avoids the discussion of whether Dad is selfish or not, what is typical or not and it keeps to the point about who is using the car.

Few things are more satisfying than seeing your children have teenagers of their own.
(Doug Larson, author)

What teenagers want

Teenagers want from their family:

- boundaries

- compromise and negotiation

- appropriate levels of responsibility for decisions

- open communication with parents

- adult reactions to adolescent problems

- consistency

- to know where they stand.

Easy, isn't? It all looks so easy on paper, but as all parents know, sometimes it really can be the hardest of hard work. Hopefully, though, these general principles will provide a bit of guidance when you're stuck and add a few bits and pieces to your general parenting arsenal.

Looking after yourself

There will be days when dealing with a moody teen is

right up there with root canal surgery on your list of 'things-I-don't-want-to-do-today' but you simply have to grin and bear it but there are also times when you really need to take it easy and look after yourself.

As a parent, it can be helpful:

1. to recognise your personal symptoms of stress.

In some, it's not sleeping, in others, it's snappiness or irritability, but whether your main symptom of stress is psychological, emotional, behavioural or a combination of all three, recognise the signs and take action.

Organise something with friends, arrange some babysitting if you can, but take time out. If things really feel like they're getting too much, arrange a consultation with a GP, or perhaps a session of alternative therapy like massage.

2. to plan breaks.

If at all possible, schedule in breaks to your routine. It can be something such as: between six and seven in the evening is Mum's time to practise her Italian, so leave her in peace; Saturday morning, Dad goes for a run, so don't ask for lifts.

If you have a partner, negotiate your timetable together to maximise the support you can offer each other.

3. to get the kids involved.

As mentioned before, involving adolescents in negotiation and planning can help them feel more adult and also means that you can palm off unwanted tasks on them in exchange for taxi services!

'If you walk the dog for me tonight, I will drop you and your friends off in town on Saturday.'

4. to involve friends and relatives.

It is important to take stress seriously. If you feel you are getting seriously harassed, involve your social network and family members.

If you're feeling socially isolated, try voluntary organisations and the Citizen's Advice Bureau (their address is at the back of the book) to see if there is any help they can offer.

A short intermission

So now we're at a point where we've looked at a variety of ways for parents to handle all the different changes that adolescents go through as well as some of the key principles involved in responding to adolescents.

In Chapter 7, we'll take a closer look at some things that, when they raise their head at home, are often looked on with dread by parents. Not to worry, they're all part of the fun of being a parent!

But before we go on, in the next chapter let's take a short intermission and sum up some of the things that we've looked at so far.

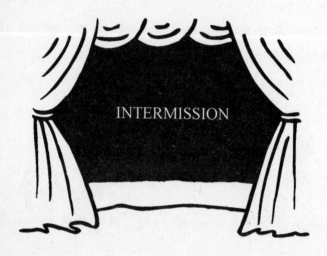

Chapter 6

To cut a long story short

The key points so far

Individual families change as their environment and circumstances change and in post-war times the composition of families has changed out of all recognition.

Nowadays, nearly twenty per cent of children live with their mother only; one in three children born to married parents witnesses their parents divorcing before the age of sixteen; mixed marriages, blending people from different cultures, are far more common; and even within the so-called 'normal family' of a mum and dad and 2.4 kids, it is quite acceptable for both parents to go out to work.

One of the biggest challenges that all families face is the onset of:

- adolescence.

Adolescence is a time of enormous physical change, preparing the adolescent for the world of adulthood. These changes involve a person becoming able to reproduce sexually and they can be embarrassing and difficult. Hormones come into play that can cause emotional upheavals. These emotional upheavals are part of developing:

- an internal world.

The internal world of an adolescent involves learning different life skills, separating from their parents and becoming an individual, making choices, decisions and mistakes.

An adolescent has to make difficult choices for the first time and learn appropriate responses and behaviours. These processes are shaped, not only by the family but also by:

- the social environment.

The adolescent's social environment involves peer groups, the media and new and more 'adult' relationships with members of the opposite sex. The social environment creates many different stresses, including academic ones.

All of these changes can cause problems, not only for the adolescent but also for the family they exist in, including their:

- parents.

Parents have to come to terms with the fact that their children are growing up and may soon be ready to leave home. They have to learn a variety of skills and techniques to try and help their adolescent become an adult and they need to have at their disposal the skills of negotiation, compromise, boundary setting and many others.

But just as no child is perfect, so no parent can be perfect either. Parents need to aim at being 'good enough' for their children, not beating themselves up for not being perfect.

And now, it's on with the show . . .

Chapter 7   Experimentation, rebellion and . . .

. . . the fun stuff that adults don't do anymore

In some ways, adolescents have it rough: all those changes and pressures, all that confusion and turmoil. On the other hand, they do get to do loads of things for the first time that are fun and exciting *and* they get away with making appalling mistakes that adults would simply not have the opportunity to make.

In this chapter, we'll look at some of the fun stuff that adolescents get to do, why they do it, what effects this can have on the family and, because I'm a stuffy old adult (it says so on my birth certificate, anyway), some of the things that can go wrong.

We'll develop this in the next chapter and look at what happens when things really do slide off the rails.

I wanted to convey a sympathetic message to both parents and children in the preceding chapters. Adolescence is tough; the old maxim goes that many people would love to go through adolescence again but with the wisdom of an adult, and that adult wisdom would be enough to convince us that once was enough, thank you very much.

But adolescence is also like being let loose in a huge social laboratory, where all sorts of fun and games are going on and we'll look at some of the pros and cons of the fun stuff in the pages that follow.

New ideas

Adolescence is a time when we are bombarded with new ideas and, without the cynicism and scepticism that many adults develop over time, fabulous new thoughts and concepts can be soaked up like water in a sponge by an adolescent; not just ideas about who they are and what they're going to do with their lives but also about wider issues that affect the planet at large.

In this period of life:

- A social conscience may develop.

- Political ideas can form.

- There is a growing sense that there is a world beyond the home town.

- Religious ideas may be questioned, adopted and discarded in a short space of time.

- Cosy adult notions about the state of the planet may be questioned.

In short, several different sets of complex ideas may be taken on with near religious fervour by individuals who, only a few years ago, were more interested in whether Barbie had ever really kissed Ken.

The conviction of these ideas can sometimes cause parents trouble. Partly this is because such ideas often change very frequently and parents can have trouble keeping up.

EXPERIMENTATION, REBELLION AND . . .

Often it is the case that ideas are defended with absolute faith (even if the proof and evidence for these ideas can be a little shaky). Furthermore, because these ideas are held so strongly, viewpoints to the contrary are often treated with disdain. Parents can be put in the position of being know-nothing-fuddy-duddies and they may feel a little bit embarrassed that their children are more informed than they are about certain things.

Lastly parents have to deal, once again, with the fact that their children are growing up.

However, these ideas are just ideas, starting points for the development of adult conversations and interests. Discussing new ideas with adolescents provides parents with another opportunity to model the appropriate skills of debate, negotiation and respect for diverse opinions – with care being taken that discussions don't become arguments!

New styles

> Don't laugh at a youth for his affectations;
> he is only trying on one face after another to
> find a face of his own.
> (Logan Pearsall Smith, 'Age and Death',
> *Afterthoughts*, 1931)

I mentioned way back in Chapter 4 the idea of adolescents identifying with things outside of themselves – in other words, adopting the speech patterns, mannerisms and dress style of other people with whom they strongly identify like pop and movie stars.

131

For an adolescent, the sense of who they are is quite new and novel – dressing or acting in a certain way is a method of saying 'Look! This is the kind of person I am!' This shorthand of identification carries on into adulthood; we can identify people as being 'like us' (or not) by the business suits they wear, by the football colours they wear on a Saturday afternoon, and so on. Adolescence is a time for experimenting with different hairdos, different make-up, different clothes and even different modes of speech.

Parents shouldn't worry too much about this; none of these choices about how to present oneself are irrevocable; hairdos can be undone, make-up can be changed and so on.

Parents of adolescent girls do have to accept that the mode of dress today is more sexual and opinions about this should be advisory – 'I'm not trying to be funny, but is this dress supposed to be that short?' – as opposed to critical – 'You're not going out looking like a street walker!' Rebellion about modes of dress does sometimes happen at school, where teachers and certain institutions sometimes have very fixed ideas about what people should wear. If your teenager says 'Well, why does it matter if I turn up to school with green hair, nose rings and red contact lenses?', they may unfortunately have a point! But as we have mentioned before, adolescents sometimes do have to do things that they don't want to do and this may well be one of those times.

Modes of speech can be introduced that are based on the culture of the day and new buzz words can come and go with alarming rapidity. Many parents complain that the phenomenon of texting has left them feeling that everybody under the age of twenty has a secret code that they have been left out of!

Make a joke of finding yourself in a situation where you're pretty sure that the people around you are talking English but it doesn't seem to make sense – 'Can you translate into English for me?' – rather than criticising or sneering. Having an adolescent in the house can be a great opportunity for parents to keep up to date on the latest trends, fashions, changing language and cultures!

Many teenagers are keen on having tattoos or piercings. It isn't legal to have these done before the age of eighteen and if someone is dead set on having them done there's not a lot you can do about it once they've hit this age. Counsel the *facts*, rather than the *fiction*!

Fact: Tattoos are permanent and yes, it does hurt to have them done.

Fact: If you get a bad tattoo and want it removed, it can cost thousands and involve painful treatment. How do you think you will feel about it in five years' time?

Fact: Piercings can become infected and people can be allergic to the metals.

Fact: Piercings to the lip and tongue can cause damage to the teeth.

Fact: If, as a teenager, you're going to have either a tattoo or a piercing: think very carefully about it; have something that will always be meaningful to you; and have it done in a reputable place with the highest standards of hygiene. *Don't do it while drunk!* It's one thing waking up at a bus stop in Leeds when you live in Lincoln; it's another to wake up at a bus stop in Leeds when you live in Lincoln with a £150-tattoo aching on your back!

Music, hobbies and passions

Adolescence is often the time when the 'soundtrack of our lives' starts to be recorded, where certain tunes have a resonance that will always be with us. It can be hard for parents to realise that some of the music that they liked is now regarded with horror and contempt by their offspring and the musical offerings that come out of a teenager's bedroom at gale force nine can leave parents shaking their head in bewilderment.

Don't fall into the trap of saying 'Music was proper music in my day.' No, it wasn't! There was some great stuff in the fifties, sixties, seventies and eighties and some utter, utter garbage as well. Take time to listen to what your children are listening to; there may well be bits that surprise you.

Negotiate what is going to be played on the house stereo and, importantly, at what volume! Many an argument about this can be short-circuited by agreeing when the volume can be creaked up. Remember, new musical technology and trends can open doors for parents as much as their children.

Hobbies can be taken up with a passion at this age, perhaps even more so than when children are a little younger. This is all part of the 'trying on of hats', the experimentation, that adolescents go through.

Be supportive and interested, share your own hobbies and interests too, but remind your adolescent that karate outfits cost money as do electric guitars – see some evidence of commitment before forking out hundreds of pounds for expensive gear!

First loves and broken hearts

> As a teenager you are at the last stage in
> your life when you will be happy to hear
> that the phone is for you.
> (Fran Lebowitz, author)

As we know from our brief tour of an adolescent's body, part of the function of puberty is to physically prepare the individual for parenthood. Before that, though, come the highs and lows of their first relationships.

Many parents look at their adolescent's early relationships with a degree of either 'Aaah, isn't that sweet' or 'Oh, God, she's not going out with that?' But we old fogies only have to look back on our own lives to remember that:

- Our early relationships were, at the time, extremely important to us.

- The feelings in these early relationships are incredibly strong.

- The ups had on us on the ceiling with happiness and the downs had on us on the floor with despair.

In short, these relationships are important in forming the basis of our views on what it is we do and do not want from future relationships. Parents need to be understanding of these relationships and treat them with respect. Privacy needs to be respected and conversations need to be had about ground rules and boundaries within the house.

If relationships seem to endure beyond the first few dates and appear to have 'legs' then make an effort to get to know the person involved; it is better to be seen by your children as someone who understands what they are going through rather than someone who is always poking their nose in or being critical of their choice.

Early relationships are also tricky for parents because they are confronted with the reality that their children are sexual beings. Teenagers do have sex – there is a reason for the tempest of hormones, remember! They usually have sex with the 'wrong' people and they often make mistakes. For some adolescents, their first sexual experience is a deep disappointment; for others, it can be fantastic. There are some things that all teenagers need to know before having sex:

- It is vital to practise 'safe sex'.

This means that both males and females should carry condoms before going to parties or on dates. This is in order to protect against sexually transmitted diseases and against unwanted pregnancy. Just as importantly, they should know how to use them – trying to put a condom on your partner with three-inch false nails would be a challenge for anyone.

- It is important to know how much alcohol they can take before their judgement is impaired.

Alcohol is usually the social lubricant of choice at parties and teenagers need to know how much they can drink before their judgement is impaired. Some teenagers do report that they don't actually

139

remember their first sexual encounter. It can be a very frightening situation to be in if you can't remember if you used protection or not.

- There can be a huge amount of peer pressure to have sex.

If adolescents do choose to have sex, it is very important that they do so because they want to rather than because they have felt pressured into doing so. A good rule of thumb seems to be:

> If you're not comfortable with it,
> don't do it.

Being able to stand up for their own choices, rather than those of their peer group, is a vital social skill for adolescents to learn.

Altered states

Western culture is heavily permeated by drugs, whether that be alcohol, tobacco, paracetamol, solvents or illegal drugs such as cannabis, ecstasy or cocaine.

Many parents experience a lot of fear and anxiety about illegal drugs but in reality alcohol is far more worrying in terms of its effects (drink-driving, violence, disinhibited behaviour) and far easier to get hold of.

The facts on drugs can be very hard for parents to get their heads around and some of the symptoms of drug use – tiredness, excitability, rapidly changing moods – are pretty common place for most teenagers whether they are using drugs or not!

141

Drug use does happen and it isn't going to go away any time soon; experimenting with altered states, whether that be through alcohol or coffee or through illegal chemicals, has been happening ever since people have been aware that it was possible.

Adolescents need to be informed about drug use, its consequences and its effects. No one should feel obliged to take something when they don't know what it is; cocaine is often cut with other adulterants, as are ecstasy and amphetamines. Cannabis, cocaine, ecstasy, heroin, LSD, magic mushrooms and amphetamines are all illegal and there are some stiff penalties that go along with possession which can have far more serious long-term consequences than the drug itself. 'I was only carrying it for my mates' doesn't hold water in court!

Any drug, illegal or legal, needs to be treated with respect. Alcohol can be a killer in excess, whether directly, through alcohol poisoning, or indirectly through drink-driving. It's very important that young people who have just passed their driving test do not think that this precious piece of paper makes them immune either to accidents or to the effects of alcohol. Getting behind the wheel of a car when you're drunk, whether you've been driving for twenty years or two months, is no longer acceptable.

Although cannabis, LSD and mushrooms can't kill, they can have profound psychological effects. Experimentation with solvents can have fatal consequences on the very first try and seventy people died in the year 2000 as a direct consequence of solvent use (as compared with the twenty-seven deaths attributed to ecstasy).

As always, it's important to be informed. There is a lot of high quality information available to both parents and teenagers from drugs agencies and they can offer confidential advice if you are worried that someone you know is using. There are also many resources on the Internet that offer information and support on problems to do with drug abuse.

143

An excellent website, where it is possible to post questions, comments or concerns anonymously, can be found at:

www.talktofrank.com

Adolescence is, then, a time of great change and great opportunity. Of course, there are going to be ups and downs, but it is worthwhile remembering that it's socially far more acceptable for seventeen-year-olds to be experimenting with new ideas, modes of dress and so on, than it is for thirty-five-year-olds. There is more leeway given to adolescents in terms of making mistakes because there is an understanding that now is the time to do it; now is the time to find out who you are and what you want from life. Parents often report that this is the period in which they see their children grow into adults – independent, with ideas and dreams of their own, making their mark on the world.

That said, it's important not to give teenagers completely free rein because, as we will see in the next chapter, things do sometimes go awry.

Chapter 8

Out of control

The serious problems that adolescents face

This chapter will look at some of the more serious problems that can arise during the adolescent years. I don't want anyone to panic on reading any of this; this chapter is written from the point of view that it's better to know what you're up against if things do go awry, rather than having something dropped on you unawares. In this chapter, we'll look at things that psychologists often deal with in their clinics, but do remember that not all adolescents present with problems in psychologists' clinics!

Because this is only a short book, we can't really examine all the serious problems that adolescents face (yep, it's another book's worth!) but we will sum up some of the major ones as well as giving some useful information and addresses at the back of the book if you need to follow up any of these ideas. Apologies are also due for the amount of technical language present in this chapter, but please don't let that put you off!

We know so far that adolescence is a time of incredible change and whenever there is great change there are often problems. Imagine moving house, changing job or starting a relationship with a new partner; there are always teething problems, difficulties, unforeseen little glitches and occasionally whopping great nightmares that accompany all these changes. Adolescence is just the same and there are the same pros and cons.

One of the big advantages of adolescence is that it is a very elastic period, and I'm not referring to money! It seems that because adolescents are bombarded with so many new experiences, their chances of recovery from negative experiences are often very good as they don't yet have patterns upon which to base judgements or predictions. In other words, adolescents are very good at picking themselves up and getting on with things. By contrast, many adults who have suffered a broken heart often say

'Right, that's it, I'll never trust anyone ever again!'

On the other hand, adolescents are also quite vulnerable, as they experience things without the filter of experience. Something bad can happen to an adolescent and they can feel overwhelmed by it instead of being able to say 'Well, this has happened before, what did I do to deal with it last time?' Adolescent naivety can be both a blessing and a curse (and so one of the important things about adolescence is to try and appear older – and therefore stronger and more resourceful – than you actually are).

We also know that it can be quite difficult to establish what is normal and what isn't for adolescents. Adolescents are prone to mood swings and emotional outbursts and therefore it can be hard for parents to know what is outside the scope of normal behaviours. Let's try and set up some general principles so that we know when to worry and when to give things a bit of time to sort themselves out.

You should be concerned:

- if the problem persists for a period of months (that is, it is chronic).

Let me translate from that little block of jargon. What I mean is this: it's very common for everybody to have periods of low mood – this is called life! If this low mood persists for a period of months and begins to affect all other areas of a person's life, then it is a problem.

For an adolescent to feel low and miserable for a week is normal and is, in fact, part of learning how to deal with negative emotions but if it goes on for a longer period of time, then help may need to be sought.

- if what is happening is snowballing.

If a problem area seems to be having a knock-on effect on other areas of a person's life, it may indicate that action needs to be taken. For example, if an adolescent experiments with graffiti with a gang of friends, this could be seen as a one-off; if the adolescent starts to truant from school to do it (so that school performance suffers) *and* gets into trouble with the law *and* starts getting into other areas of minor criminal activity then the problem has escalated and needs to be addressed.

- if the behaviour is markedly different from that of a peer group.

A psychologist colleague of mine had a referral for a young boy who was crying before he went to school, couldn't separate from his mother when she dropped him off and demanded to sleep with his mum and dad at night because he was scared of the dark. This would have been an age-appropriate problem for a six or seven-year-old boy, but not for a seventeen-year-old six-footer!

Many behaviours go on in peer groups that parents are horrified by, but they may well be normal for that particular group. However, if a behaviour is markedly different from what most other adolescents are doing at that age, then perhaps help needs to be sought.

Let's now take a closer look at some examples of adolescent problems.

Mental health

Depression

Adolescent moods are often longer and more pronounced than those experienced by people in general since adolescents are in the process of learning how to regulate and cope with their feelings. However, depression is more serious that just a bad mood and, if it has been going on for a period of months, it is important to seek help.

Parents often say 'They're only sixteen! What have they got to be depressed about?' However, this sort of comparison is not really helpful. You may remember the Monty Python film, *Life of Brian*, in which our hero finds himself assaulted, spat upon and thrown into a murky cell by a Roman. Just as our hero is starting to feel sorry for himself, his cell mate remarks 'You lucky *bleep*! Right little centurion's pet, aren't you?' Deal with the feelings, rather than trying to assess whether someone deserves to have them!

Depression is often marked by:

- depressed behaviours such as a marked lack of interest in things that previously brought enjoyment

- a lack of self-care

- excessive sleeping (although please note that your adolescent sleeping until three in the afternoon shouldn't be regarded as a cause for worry in and of itself!)

- depressed thoughts, and a negative view of the world, the self and the future

- depressed feelings (psychologists sometimes refer to something called the 'flattened affect' – in other words, the normal range of emotions seems somehow dull and flat).

Such symptoms, if they persist, warrant specialist attention. Talk to your child and explain that you are worried and concerned for them. There might be an underlying problem that they are unwilling to talk about with you, so find out if they have anyone else to talk to about it, whether that be a best friend or other confidant. Talk to your GP if the problem goes on and if you are not reassured, seek a referral to a Child and Adolescent Community Mental Health Team.

Do consult your adolescent throughout this process and reassure them that you don't think they're crazy, but that you do want to see them being their 'old selves' again.

Parents sometimes worry that they can't 'push' their adolescent if they are depressed, for fear that they may threaten self-harm (such as cutting themselves) or even suicide. Adolescents do threaten suicide and because you know your children better than anyone, it's important to be able to distinguish between 'They didn't have the dress I wanted in my size! I'm going to kill myself!' and something that seems to have a ring of despair. Treat any such comments seriously: talk to your child and tell them how worried such comments make you; and contact your GP if you believe that something out of the ordinary is going on. If you are the parent of a teenager who has suggested that they might hurt themselves or kill themselves, it is an impossible burden to shoulder alone and professionals do need to be involved.

Anxiety disorders

Anxiety is not a problem in and of itself; in fact, some anxiety is necessary if we are going to do well at a job interview or exam. But sometimes, anxiety can start to interfere with (instead of helping) performance. If anxiety is interfering with a person's enjoyment of life, then it might be an idea to seek help. However, it should be noted that people can live with anxiety disorders for many years that only affect one area of their life and still be extremely happy; the footballer Dennis Berkamp is phobic of flying (and has done pretty well for himself!) and many actors and musicians refer to stage fright so severe that it caused them to be physically sick. Specific anxiety, that is, anxiety related to a single, specific cause, such as exams, can be helped with simple relaxation techniques.

Shyness is very common in adolescents, especially when talking to the opposite sex, but social phobia often involves outright avoidance of many social situations. This can impede an adolescent's development, especially at a time when social contacts and development are very important. As we mentioned above, one important thing to consider when wondering whether to seek help or whether to give the problem a bit of time, is the extent to which a person's life is being interfered with.

Obsessive Compulsive Disorder (OCD)

Obsessive Compulsive Disorder, often referred to as OCD, is characterised by obsessions (thoughts that won't go away) and compulsions (the need to carry out certain behaviours based on these thoughts).

Again, remember that most people have quirks and eccentricities; but if these interfere with a person's daily routine then help can be sought. For example, most of us check the gas before we leave the house but if we're checking it fifty times before we go out so that we are late for school and can't meet friends, then it becomes a problem.

Eating disorders

I spent the first fourteen years of my life convinced that my looks were hideous. Adolescence is painful for everyone, I know,but mine was plain weird.

(Uma Thurman)

Adolescence is the peak age of onset for eating disorders and girls are significantly more affected than boys. We live in a culture that is dominated by physical appearance, fad diets, calorie counting and a strong preoccupation with body image. An eating disorder is really any or all of these things taken to extremes.

155

In girls, anorexia can severely impede normal development (periods can stop and the development of secondary sexual characteristics can be interfered with) because the body simply lacks the energy for all of the necessary biological processes. Anorexia involves a host of different problems, but all centre around food and eating, for example:

- obsession with body image and diet

- marked loss of weight

- restriction of food intake

- compulsive exercise

- distortion of body image (seeing oneself as fat when in fact one is very underweight).

Anorexia can be a life-threatening condition and requires medical and psychological intervention. As usual, your GP is your first point of call.

At the other end of the eating disorders' scale is obesity. Although there are a very few people for whom there is a genetic predisposition towards obesity, in general there is a simple equation: if the amount of exercise you do is outweighed by the number of calories you are eating, then you will put on weight. If this goes on for long periods of time, then problems can occur: the load placed on the heart and other body systems causes them to be strained, muscles and joints can suffer, and a vicious cycle is established.

This vicious cycle can involve someone using food for comfort in the same way that another person might use drugs; unfortunately, if the thing that gives you great comfort is also the thing that causes you terrible problems, it can be difficult to find new ways and new things to give you that comfort.

Furthermore, particularly in adolescence, where body image is so important, being very overweight can play havoc on a developing self-image and many overweight adolescents refer to bullying and name calling, which, in themselves, can become very difficult problems for people to deal with. The keys are sensible diet and sensible exercise regimens; that may involve getting rid of the PlayStation for a few months and no pocket money for McDonalds.

Behavioural problems

Behavioural problems in adolescence have attracted a huge amount of media attention recently and the British government has tried to tackle some of the more serious problems with Anti-Social Behaviour Orders (ASBOs), tagging and exclusion orders. Time will tell if these really work.

As we know, adolescence is a time when norms for behaviour are worked out, moral codes established and boundaries set up. It's perfectly normal for adolescents to have outbursts and temper tantrums, but left unchecked, behavioural problems can cause severe impairments in their academic, social and psychological progress. There really is a huge difference between adolescents who are naughty and cause the odd problem and those who are really out of control and seem to be unable to respect the most basic social norms.

Oppositional Defiant Disorder (ODD)

Broadly speaking, psychologists often divide the 'anti-social behaviours' seen so often in the press into two categories: Oppositional Defiant Disorder (ODD) and Conduct Disorders (CD). ODD is regarded as 'milder' although some of the symptoms can be extremely difficult for parents to deal with. They include:

- negative and hostile behaviour

- loss of temper and constant arguing

- refusal to accede to adult requests

- spiteful, vindictive behaviour

- ability to recognise the rules but difficulties in internalising them and acting upon them.

No doubt virtually all parents will say 'A-ha! So that's why they act like that!' But remember what we said earlier: these symptoms must be present for an extended period of time and cause major problems in normal functioning.

Conduct Disorders (CD)

CD is often regarded as much more severe than ODD, although on a similar continuum. Often people who are diagnosed with CD have some involvement with the police services as their actions exceed what might be called 'occasional lawbreaking'. Its features involve:

- bullying, fighting, use of weapons

- cruelty to animals

- destruction or damage to property

- theft

- truancy or repeated incidents of running away from home.

Again, it is important to remember that for a proper diagnosis of either of these conditions, the difficulties must have been present for a period of six months; there is a world of difference between someone who steals from a shop and feels enormous guilt and regret and who, as a consequence of this, decides that stealing is not for them and a person who steals frequently with little or no remorse. Both ODD and CD (and more especially CD) are serious conditions and help should be sought. As always, your GP is your 'gateway' to service.

Truancy

Many children 'bunk off' school once or twice; problems arise when this interferes with their academic performance or masks a deeper problem. It's important not to panic if you receive a call from your adolescent's school to tell you that they haven't been attending when they should have been and to address the problem calmly.

This can be especially important if a child is truanting because they are being bullied and school has become a negative experience. It can also sometimes be the case that truancy is occurring because an adolescent is finding the academic demands of school to be too much, which can occur when the academic demands of school increase. It is possible to cover up academic problems in junior

161

school, perhaps by clowning around but when the academic demands become more severe, rather than admitting that they are struggling, some adolescents simply stop attending.

Careful liaison with the school is advisable and it's important to involve adolescents in any programme that the school recommends in order to effect a return to school. It is important to take truancy seriously, as the school terms do whizz by and academic progress can be impeded.

Chapter 9 Problems not of their own making

Domestic violence

Adolescents do cause their parents sleepless nights, but it's never all one way traffic. Children can suffer because of the arguments, rows and conflicts that their parents have.

Space doesn't permit a lengthy analysis of this, but it is a sad fact of life that in today's world, many people (the vast proportion of them women) suffer violence, whether that be physical or verbal, at the hands of their partner.

Children are *always* affected by this and sometimes the consequences do not show up until years later. Children have the right to be protected from violence and help must be sought if this is an issue at home. Violence is unacceptable at home, is never an excuse and must not be tolerated.

Divorce

Despite their best intentions, parents do break up and households do split up. Many adults like to pretend that their divorce was a cordial affair that had little or no impact on their children. They often assume that their adolescents have understood what has been happening and that they are coping just fine. This is unfortunately highly illogical.

If you have ever been divorced, you will know yourself what a difficult process it can be, how emotions can be tangled up and savaged, how it is difficult from one moment to the next to know what is happening and how painful even the most civilised divorce can be. Obviously, there are also the logistics of the whole affair: who is moving where, who is getting the house, the stereo, the dog – and where the kids are going to be living.

While all this adult conflict is going on, children can find themselves caught in the middle of it and it can be a hugely difficult time for them.

Try to bear in mind certain general principles:

- Your problems are your own; don't involve your children in trying to resolve parental issues.

- Arguments happen but if possible, keep them out of the faces of your children.

- Do, however, keep your children involved in what is going on. They live with you and have a right to know their future, even if you're uncertain. Tell them that you're uncertain, reinforce that they are not to blame and that you will both love them whatever happens.

- Don't 'triangulate' – in other words, don't try and make your children allies against the other parent, however tempting that might be.

Connected with the effects of divorce on children are three related issues, which are explored below:

- bereavement in adolescence

- single parenthood

- stepfamilies.

Bereavement in adolescence

Bereavement, or loss, can come in many forms. People can experience these feelings as a result of the death of a loved one, the breaking up of a family, a loss of income, or the loss of friendship groups as a result of a moving to a new school.

In this section, I'll focus on the effects of losing a parent through death and talk about the effects of separation and readjustment in the section on stepfamilies.

The death of a loved one is a highly traumatic event at the best of times and can be especially hard on the young adolescent who is only beginning to come to terms with the concept of death, never mind its personal meaning.

The sudden death of a parent through an accident or heart attack is, in many ways, far more traumatic than the death of a parent as a result of a protracted illness as there has been no time to prepare the child for what has happened.

Some research suggests that where there is time to prepare an adolescent for such an event some reorganisation of the meaning systems for children can take place and they can be forewarned.

As well as their still-undeveloped sense of what death actually means, the other confounding problem for adolescents can be that it is obviously highly traumatic for a parent to lose their partner and therefore extremely difficult for the surviving parent to prioritise support for their children in the face of their own grief. It is therefore vital that the surviving parent acknowledge their own grief and pain before trying to help their children with theirs.

Research suggests that bereavement in adolescence can be helped by the following factors:

- a secure and stable relationship with the parent prior to their death

- prompt, accurate information about what has happened being given to the child

- the child being allowed to ask questions, seek information and participate in family grieving rituals, funerals

- assurances from the surviving parent that this relationship will go on.

Regardless of the age of the adolescent, it is necessary to discuss with them what has happened while, at the same time, making it clear that they are not responsible for the grief of the surviving parent.

The surviving parent must seek the help that they need from friends, family and, if necessary, the appropriate services. Comforting an older adolescent can be harder because their newly formed coping strategies have suddenly had to undergo an incredibly harsh test and they may lash out in anger. This lashing out is not personal, but an expression of the rage they feel at the unfairness of it all.

The loss, through death, of a parent and partner creates a time of emotional shock and reorganisation within the family that needs to be handled with extreme sensitivity and care.

Bereavement is a process that plays out slowly, day on day, moment to moment and it cannot be rushed or forced. The scarring that it causes can also create strength in the knowledge that, even against the harshest tests, life does go on.

There are many symptoms of bereavement that are commonplace and need to be handled with care and compassion. The school also needs to be involved in creating a protective framework around the child. Whilst going through the stages of grief, many adolescents experience the following problems:

- 'Accelerated maturity' and trying to be a 'pseudo-adult'.

This may in turn lead to an adolescent trying to parent the surviving parent, which can complicate and confuse the roles in the family – the adolescent needs to carry on with the tasks of adolescence, not the tasks of parenting.

- Anger.

Anger and the feeling that 'there is no point to anything, anymore' may in turn lead to anti-social behaviours, as the adolescent tries to block out what has happened.

- Temporary drops in school performance and attendance.
- Temporary withdrawal from social spheres and accompanying loss of self-esteem.

- Temporary problems with sleeping, low mood, reduction in food intake.

The last three symptoms are very similar to the symptoms of depression, and grief can change into a depressive illness if the grieving process is blocked.

- Fear of losing the surviving parent and longing for the lost parent.

All of the symptoms listed above are normal and accompany the grieving process. However, this process, like any other, can go wrong and result in something known as 'complicated grief'.

Complicated grief occurs when the grief process becomes blocked or extended; depressive symptoms are standard in the first few months after a bereavement but if they are still as intense and painful after a year as they were after a few days, this is suggestive that the process has gone awry.

Contact with your GP (either for your children or for yourself) is necessary if you want to unblock this process. It is a testament to the power of the human spirit that recovery can take place; the process of bereavement is one of healing but it does take time.

Being part of a single-parent family

A parent may become the sole provider and lone carer of their child(ren) as a consequence of either bereavement or separation.

This can lead to a period of immense stress, as the family system has to reorganise and change while still going about its daily business and routines. It can take a long time to come to terms with the process of adjustment from being a couple to being a single parent; even if the previous relationship has ended badly, it can be a long time before a sense of 'all is well' can be experienced.

Practical issues

When a family becomes a single-parent family, there can be significant changes in:

1. Income.

If a family has been so arranged that the father has gone out to work and the mother has stayed at home, then it will be very difficult for the mother, in the short term, to make up the sudden shortfall in income.

2. Who does what in the family.

If a father who has previously gone out to work suddenly becomes the sole care giver, then there can be a period in which he has to learn skills that have previously been carried out by the mother: looking after the children when they are sick, attending parents' evenings and so on. Older adolescents

173

often become more involved in some of the day-to-day running of the household, which they can resent. It is important that adolescents are allowed to be adolescents, rather than, as mentioned above, pseudo-adults.

3. Location.

If a house has to be sold on, then the family has to come to terms with what will happen to their family home and who gets what. Coupled with changes in family income, this loss of status as a homeowner can be hard to come to terms with.

Emotional needs

As well as the practical issues that have to be addressed, there are also the emotional needs of the family members to be considered. As I mentioned before in the section on divorce, it's important for parents to accept that, although they may have a great deal of anger, resentment and sadness towards their former partner (regardless of how the separation has come about) it is necessary to avoid running down the non-resident parent.

Recent research asking children about their needs and wants has made it clear that children do not want to be involved in their parents' disputes; they want their non-resident parent to be as reliable and consistent as possible (where possible) and to have someone available to them who they trust and to whom they can talk (perhaps a member of the extended family).

The organisation Gingerbread can provide help as well as a wealth of information and support for lone parent families.

Single fathers

A lot of recent media attention has focussed on single fathers and their role in society. Lone fathers state that the following issues can be difficult to cope with at first:

- the shock of a sudden shift in roles

- being perceived as 'odd' because you are a father as a sole parent

- loneliness and isolation.

175

It can be worth bearing in mind that around eleven per cent of all single parents who have sole responsibility for their child(ren) are men and that this is becoming more and more common.

Characteristically, men are seen as being 'less emotional' and 'not as good as women about talking about emotions', but this is part of the sudden shift in roles that single fathers have to learn to cope with.

They must involve their children in what is happening and explain why the situation is like it is, just as single mothers have to do. They must also learn to be sensitive to the stigma that is still placed on the children of single parents (although this is far less prevalent than it was).

Being part of a stepfamily

When a parent begins a relationship with a new partner, the model for this new relationship is often based on their past relationships. However, a vital step towards a harmonious home life is accepting that stepfamilies are completely different from biological families; there are difficulties to be faced which are different from those faced by biological families.

Firstly, in a relationship where there are no children, the couple get to carry out their courtship and form their relationship independently. Whereas in a step-family, this has to happen while there are already children present, adding considerably to the stress of forming a relationship with a new partner.

Furthermore, there are in-built comparisons that take place, especially when the children are older adolescents. For example, having a teenager around who says 'My Mum/Dad wouldn't do it like that' can present a real challenge to the most resilient step-parent. Developing alternative parenting strategies will take time and much patience on the part of both parent and step-parent.

One of the biggest difficulties with stepfamilies is that they suffer from numerous myths that simply don't hold water – consider the role played by the wicked stepmother in fairy tales!

Common myths that adults have about a stepfamily may need to be addressed before the idea of all moving in together takes place, namely:

- The members of a stepfamily should all love one another.

Why? Moving in with people who you've only just met is a difficult task regardless of the circumstances; asking children to do it (perhaps while they're just trying to establish their own independence) can be extremely difficult. Stepparents can also be horribly disappointed when their best efforts to be loving and caring towards their new stepchildren go unreciprocated.

- The adults will love each other enough to overcome any obstacle.

Love doesn't conquer all; if you're relying solely on love to get you through then it's likely you're going to be sorely disappointed. The fact that there will be several months of teething troubles has to be accepted by all concerned, otherwise stepfamilies can tear themselves apart before they've had a chance to come together.

• The non-resident biological parent can be assimilated easily into a stepfamily in some capacity.

Ideally, this will happen but all too often, it won't. Adults get jealous and angry that their ex-partner has started a new relationship. Children can feel isolated from their non-resident parent, which can, in turn, lead to blaming of the new step-parent.

Research has suggested that stepfamilies often go through a period of reorganisation which involves several different stages. The first stage is often called fantasy, where there is a stage of believing that all will be well in the world (a 'honeymoon' phase). At this stage in the process, families do not believe that changes need to be made.

This is often followed by a stage of panic where the family realises that it does in fact, need to change and reorganise. This is often accompanied by feelings of blame and accusations. It seems that the younger the children are, the easier this process is.

The third stage can be labelled chaos! During this phase, radical reorganisations take place and the family starts to move and change. It can be a difficult time for all concerned, but it is necessary for the new heads of the family to pull together and remember why they came together in the first place.

A stepfamily that emerges, blinking at the light, from this stage can move into phases of stability and progress. Member of this new unit become open to accepting change and accustomed to the new patterns, problem-solving techniques and ideas of the new family unit.

Once a family moves through these stages, they can then come to accept some of the positives of this experience: a tolerance of different lifestyles, an acceptance of difference, new social experiences and the birth of a new, successful family.

Don't despair and don't suffer alone

The problems outlined in this chapter can be absolutely devastating for families and very difficult for them to cope with and can really put into perspective how difficult the adolescent years can be.

These problems are not resolvable overnight, no matter how much families wish they could be and professional services in this country are badly overloaded but it's important to remember that you don't have to suffer alone.

Get professional services involved, get the school on your side and involve your friends and relatives. Don't feel embarrassed or ashamed, but do try to resolve the problem before it gets any worse.

It's an important message to give to families that, no matter what, don't despair. Situations do change, problems do get resolved.

PROBLEMS NOT OF THEIR OWN MAKING

Looking at some of the problems we have explored in this chapter, it can be amazing that families do cope, but cope they do and getting through serious situations does say something very important about the resilience of family members and the feelings that they have for each other.

I hope you're still with me! Let's take a deep breath and plunge into Chapter 10.

Chapter 10   Troubleshooting
problems at home

Lost in translation

Welcome to the last chapter of the book! I applaud your persistence and hope that you've found some interesting bits and pieces to pick up and investigate along the way. If you're worried about where to look next and what to do, don't worry, there's a host of useful information in the Appendix of the book – addresses, websites, books – all manner of helpful hints to add depth and breadth to what we've covered here. Let's summarise some of the things we've looked at already before adding the finishing touches.

What characterises adolescence?

- enormous physical, psychological, social and academic change

As adults know, when change comes along, there can be 'pressure points' or areas that are more vulnerable to going 'out of sync'.

- boundary-testing, trying on different identities, testing adult authority and values

- making mistakes, some big, some small, with the aim of gaining experience and finding out for oneself what life is all about

- experimentation, new ideas, new theories, new music (and fun!)

- new relationships, including sexual ones, and preparation for adulthood.

In the cold light of day, it's easy to be sympathetic to adolescents who are going through all this stuff. When you're living with it twenty-four hours a day, seven days a week, year in, year out (sorry to remind you!), it can be extremely hard to keep a lid on your own feelings and be balanced and fair.

As everybody knows, it's far easier to give advice to other people about their problems than to give (and follow) sound advice to yourself. So why not try the little thought experiment below?

THOUGHT EXPERIMENT 2
Imagine they were someone else's

Aah, if only . . . It can be helpful at times of stress to take a step back from the problem and try to imagine it through a different perspective. Imagine your offspring has been spawned by someone else.

What would their good qualities be? Their bad ones? If you were giving advice to someone about this person, what would you say? How would you describe this person's pressure points? What skills do they have to get through this particular period? What would you say are the best ways to approach this person? Do they respond to praise and reinforcement or do they like to be more firmly motivated? Who are their friends and social helpers?

Imagining that your child is someone's else's can sometimes unblock repetitive patterns that can be unhelpful in families. Thinking about things from a slightly different perspective can really help a situation that feels 'stuck'.

Try different modes of communication if you want to say something to your children and speech just doesn't seem to be working: write a letter, send an email or arrange to do something nice and special with them.

Four key life skills

Adolescents have learnt a whole host of skills from their parents that their parents might not even be aware of. When children are younger, they begin to learn important life skills like sharing, cooperation and so on; they learn to share their toys with younger siblings, to not interrupt people when they're on the phone, and to not stick bogies on the windows or insert jam sandwiches in the video because it looked hungry.

Adolescents apply these skills on a much wider scale and on a much broader canvas. Let's take a closer look at four key life skills that are both learnt and applied in adolescence and that are critical to becoming a successful and prosperous adult:

- negotiating wants and desires
- establishing and respecting boundaries
- developing trust
- accepting responsibility.

Negotiating wants and desires

Did your parents ever say to you 'I want, never gets?' This little gem of wisdom implies that people have to wait for what they want; they don't have a God-given right to get it.

Patience and negotiating with other people who may have different goals and interests from you is a desperately important skill to learn and people don't get far in life without it. If you order your adolescent to do something without explaining why but 'Because I say so!', it's difficult for them to learn that in the world outside the home this doesn't always work: try telling a university admissions panel or a job interview group that you should get the place at uni or the job 'Because I say so!'

Establishing and respecting boundaries

Teenagers often go a bit wild at university and the standard lament is because 'My parents never gave me any freedom at home.'

All teenagers say this, even if they lived in a private granny flat at the end of the garden. However, many teenagers find that the boundaries that their parents gave them are the ones that they eventually come to accept (when it becomes OK to say that your parents did some good things).

Boundaries around general behaviour, moral behaviour and even sexual behaviour are established at home and with a peer group. Boundaries help social cooperation and social groups to function.

Anyone who has lived in a university hall of residence will know that it's a far more pleasant place to live in if there's been some sort of agreement that leaving plates, dishes and cups for so long in the sink that they start *to grow things* is not fair to the rest of the people trying to use that sink.

And that setting off fireworks at three in the morning on a regular basis is not acceptable!

Boundaries need to be covertly or overtly agreed upon so that there are no arguments about them. Parents therefore need to be relatively firm with their boundaries but they also need to cooperate with their adolescents when it comes to establishing them.

Developing trust

A classic parental response is 'You can have your ball back when you've learnt how to play with it.' How do you learn how to play with it if someone's taken it away? How do you learn to come back home at midnight if you've been grounded? Trust is hugely important and all human relationships flounder without it.

Whether they know it or not, adolescents come to trust that their parents have their best interests at heart and relationships in which this trust has been broken are notoriously difficult to repair. Allow for one-offs – fifteen minutes late home does not constitute grounds for eviction – but do foster this trust by explaining why it's so important.

Accepting responsibility

Hand in hand with trust goes responsibility. Adolescents have to deal with an increased amount of responsibility: academic, social and financial. You're not doing your children any favours if you seek to take that responsibility away from them because they're 'growing up too fast'. Negotiate with them about pocket money; negotiate with them on areas of responsibility around the house. Negotiate, negotiate . . .

. . . and negotiate!

191

Responsibility is something that everyone has to get used to and it can involve having to do things that people just don't want to do. Life is tough!

While all of this is going on, it's perhaps no surprise that the commonest lament among both parents and adolescents is 'They just don't understand me!' Let's take a closer look at why this might be.

'THEY JUST DON'T UNDERSTAND ME'
(an adolescent's point of view)

'My folks are OK, I suppose. I know other kids have it worse, but there's just so much that does my head in. Like, the other day, I was getting ready to go out to see John. We've only been together for a few weeks, but he's really nice, dead cool.

'Anyway, it's taken me ages to get my hair right, cos I've got this really cool new cut and just as I'm ready to go out, Mum's on at me to get the rubbish out. I said I'll do it later and she just went nuts, going on about how I've got my responsibilities and all this heavy stuff. It's only the rubbish.

'Anyway, I was out of the door by this point, I'm not taking any of her stress. She's just frustrated because her and Dad had a row the other night about him going to football too often or something. Dad's being a real pain at the moment, just cos he hates his job and can't be bothered to find something else. He's always going on about how I'm so lucky and I don't know I'm born. Yeah, right. I've got exams next year, homework coming out of my ears, my best friend Chrissie's got anorexia and she's phoning me up all the time.

'And Phil, my little brother, is being a pain, too. Whenever John calls, he's making these stupid faces and jokes and stuff and Mum and Dad just let him do it! He was even in my room the other day. "Oh, he's only ten, leave him alone!" Well, I'm only fifteen, why don't they leave me alone?

Why don't they understand me?'

Timing and moods

The little monologue above illustrates a couple of additional points:

- timing

- moods.

Timing

You know how annoying it is when your children say, just as they're about to leave for school, 'Oh, by the way, Dad, I need picking up from the Sports Centre at eight tonight because I'm playing football and I could do with ten pounds because we're going to get a burger first and have you signed that permission form for me and I need that shirt ironed, thanks, bye!'

Well, it's the same for adolescents. Anticipation is important for parents, a skill you all learnt when you were dealing with a toddler – what looks like a table to you is an irresistible assault course for a toddler with many opportunities to injure themselves. Anticipate things, give a gentle reminder the day before you need something done.

Moods

Your children may not appreciate your moods. We've talked a bit about teenage moods; adult moods can be just as bad and often go on for longer. Parents are sometimes caught between not wanting to involve their children too much in their problems (correct!) and wanting to be emotionally honest around their kids (also correct!).

A balance needs to be struck and sometimes some sort of shorthand developed to communicate that things are not bright and shiny all the time for Mum and Dad. It's not on for teenagers to inflict their moods on everybody else (although they will); try not to inflict yours on them and apologise if you do!

I hope the all of the above illustrates something we mentioned at the beginning – adolescents don't live in a vacuum; they live in a complex web of systems that involve different people with different personalities who all want different things. It's a tricky juggling act.

Now, just to prove how even-handed and balanced I am (just kidding), we'll have a look at things from the other side of the fence.

TROUBLESHOOTING PROBLEMS AT HOME

'THEY JUST DON'T UNERSTAND ME'
(a parent's point of view)

'Of course, I love my kids, there's no doubt about that. But, my God, they're a handful. Phil's only ten and he's just getting to that cheeky age, and Claire's fifteen, so of course she knows it all bigger and better than everybody.

'I know it winds my husband Mike up no end to hear Claire talking sometimes about how tough her life is and he's working in that horrible job just to pay for all the stuff that kids think they have to have these days.

'And sometimes she's just so disrespectful!

'I couldn't believe it, the other day when I asked her to take out the rubbish. We all agreed that would be her job and she didn't seem to mind – it's hardly backbreaking work. But she was in a rush and she shouted at me when I asked her! Told me I should just get off her back and stop hassling her! And then when she comes back and I tell her that's not on, she has another go at me for bringing up stuff 'from the past!' But I bet all will be sweetness and light when she next needs a lift or some cash.

'Sometimes I don't know where my daughter has gone. She's been replaced by this demanding toddler who always wants her own way. I thought they were supposed to get more mature as they get older, not less! And it's not as if I'm a dragon – I always try and explain my point of view.

Why doesn't she understand me?'

Another two important points

This little parental snippet illustrates another two important points (and I haven't included what Mike, the father, or Phil, the little brother, think – that's right, it's another book!):

• Adolescents are just passing through.

The comment that adolescence is just a phase is, to

some extent, accurate; adolescents are in the process of leaving the exit marked 'childhood' and searching for the turn-off to 'adulthood'. It's only natural that they should flip between the two from time to time!

• Adolescents have selective memories.

I once nearly caused my mother to have an aneurysm when I told her I remembered being a calm, mature adolescent! Most adolescents feel that their behaviour is reasonable because they are still pretty egocentric – they still do believe that the world, to some extent, revolves around them. This changes with time (usually, although I haven't dared tell my mum that I remember being a calm twenty-five-year-old) as they come to find their place in the sun.

> When I was a boy of fourteen, my father
> was so ignorant I could hardly stand to have the
> old man around. But when I got to be twenty-one,
> I was astonished at how much he had
> learned in seven years.
> (Mark Twain, author)

No family is perfect!

So there you have it. In any family, there are always causes for complaint and for improvement, but as a closing note, it's important to remember that *no* family is perfect.

The joke in clinical psychology is that the family members who say at the first meeting 'It's not me . . . I'm the normal one!' are often (all right, always) the most difficult!

Being odd, strange or weird as a family is nothing to be ashamed about; if you manage to get right most of the things that we talked about earlier (successful families do, and you do most of the time) you're doing extremely well.

No adolescent is perfect either but, even if they don't say it, adolescents do love their parents even if there is all out war some of the time. They are linked to their family by blood and no tie is stronger. It can be helpful to remember these fundamentals when things are strained.

And with that cheery note ringing in your ears, I will take my leave. I hope this book has been helpful to you. There are more goodies in the final section of the book to steer you in the right direction if you want further help.

Enjoy your kids, help them to enjoy their teenage years and the very best of luck!

Appendix The stuff that wouldn't
fit anywhere else

Contact details and websites

All the contact information, websites and Internet addresses given in this section were current, correct and active as of October 2006 – apologies if any of them have changed between the book being finished and the book being published.

If you don't have access to the Internet, go along to your local central library, most of which now have free access.

Surveys and books

Top ten parental worries survey

There has been a lot of interesting survey research carried out on adolescents and the issues that affect them, much of it by the BBC. One interesting survey was about what parents worry about. Before you have a look at the list on the next page, have a think about what would your Top Ten parental worries be.

The poll found that the Top Ten parental worries were of their children:

1. being hit by a car

2. being abducted or murdered

3. eating too much sweet stuff

4. spending too much time watching TV or playing computer games

5. growing up too fast

6. being a victim of crime

7. eating too much junk food

8. being badly influenced by friends

9. getting a serious illness

10. being the victim of physical violence.

If you'd like to find out more about this survey, try the book that produced the results by Paul Martin and Kristina Murrin – it's called *The 50 Most Common Concerns of Parents Explored and Explained*.

So there are another forty worries for you to look at!

BBC teens survey

Some BBC surveys published a couple of years ago have some interesting results too. Have a look at the following website:

http://www.bbc.co.uk/suffolk/dont_miss/2003/10/
teens/features/survey.shtml#key

Research Machines survey

An excellent survey, full of information, was carried out by the group Research Machines and was quoted by the Teacher Support Network. Have a look at the results at:

http://www.teacherline.org.uk/index.cfm?p=1814

Two useful books

A useful, down-to-earth book is *Whatever! A Down-to-earth Guide to Parenting Teenagers* by Gill Hines and Alison Baverstock and many parents have found that Bill Watterson's *Calvin and Hobbes* is full of spot-on comments about parenting, even if Calvin is only six and Hobbes is a tiger!

Not Another Self-help Book

Shameless plug department: if you liked this book, my first was called *Not Another Self-help Book* from the same publishers. It's a light-hearted book aimed at helping people get over some of the self-defeating thoughts that we're all prone to.

You can also find articles that I've written in *My Weekly* magazine, published by DC Thomson, and back copies are available from them. Plug over!

General information and help

Childline

A useful telephone number for teenagers is at Childline on:

0800 1111

If a teenager feels that they have no one to talk to about a particular issue, this is the number to call for excellent advice and help.

The Childline website can be found at:

www.childline.org.uk

On that website is some useful information about bullying. Childline's night service is in desperate trouble due to lack of funds and if you want to help keep Childline open 24 hours a day have a look at their website to see how you can help.

Citizens Advice

The Citizens Advice's website is at:

www.citizensadvice.org.uk

Citizens Advice have advice and information about all sorts of different topics in Citizens Advice Bureaux across the UK with a specific focus on what's going on in your local area.

They have also recently published a book, the *Citizens Advice Handbook*, which has information on a huge range of topics.

Parentline Plus

Parentline Plus is another useful website for parents, offering advice and support. They can be contacted on:

Freephone 0808 800 2222

On their website, you can find a whole host of useful addresses and contact numbers on a variety of subjects. You can also access their confidential email service on their website,. Their website is at:

www.parentlineplus.org.uk

The Samaritans

If you want some confidential advice and support when you've reached the end of your tether – and this is for parents and adolescents – you can contact the Samaritans by phone on:

08457 909090

You can also write, in confidence, to Chris at PO Box 9090, Stirling, FK8 2SA, or by email to:

jo@samaritans.org

Gingerbread

Gingerbread is a support organisation for over 2.5 million single parents and their children throughout England and Wales. Their website is at:

www.gingerbread.org.uk

Their advice service can be contacted at:

Freephone 0800 018 4318

or by email at:

advice@gingerbread.org.uk

Specific help on specific topics

Anxiety disorders

A useful web page containing useful links to other relevant web sites can be found at:

http://www.keepkidshealthy.com/welcome/
conditions/anxiety_disorders.html

It's a little bit technical but covers all the important bases.

Depression

A useful web page from the Psychology Information Online service, which gives short, useful information and advice about depression, can be found at:

www.psychologyinfo.com/depression/teens.htm#teen
-depression

Do remember that your GP practice will often have useful info, too.

Cathy Richards, Eileen Scott and Nicky Cannon have produced an excellent online resource about depression in teenagers and it can be found at:

www.depressioninteenagers.co.uk

It is an extremely useful resource that covers everything from the causes of depression to stories from teenagers who have suffered from it.

Domestic violence

Possibly the best resource for this subject is at:

http://www.womensaid.org.uk

The helpline for this organisation is on:

Freephone 0808 2000 247

Call if you have any queries or worries. There is also a confidential email service at:

helpline@womensaid.org.uk

Drugs

The following three websites are very helpful in providing useful and reliable information.

1.   www.talktofrank.com

This website has some excellent, down-to-earth advice and info about drugs.

You can also call this organisation on:

0800 776600

or email them with queries at:

frank@talktofrank.com

2.   www.erowid.org

This website is packed with useful information about drugs, their legality and their significance.

3.   www.tdpf.org.uk

The Transform Drug Policy Foundation has some excellent resources about the government's drug policy, with sensible and well-argued debate about whether the policy works in reducing drug use. An excellent site if you want to have an intelligent debate about the subject.

Eating disorders

The Eating Disorders Association (EDA) has a confidential Youthline for people up to the age of eighteen. Call them on:

0845 634 7650

Their website can be found at:

www.edauk.com

And their postal address is EDA, 103 Prince of Wales Road, Norwich, NR1 1DW.

Education

The Advisory Centre for Education (ACE) can be contacted via their website at:

www.ace-ed.org.uk

ACE offers advice in relation to virtually every topic

affecting children between the ages of five and sixteen in state education in England and Wales, such as bullying, school exclusion and special educational needs. Their general advice line (Monday to Friday, 2–5 pm) is at:

Freephone 0808 800 5793

Sexual health

Brook Advisory Centres – commonly known just as Brook – is the only national voluntary sector provider of free and confidential sexual health advice and services specifically for young people under twenty-five. Brook is a registered charity, and has forty years' experience of providing professional advice through specially trained doctors, nurses, counsellors and outreach and information workers to over 100,000 young people each year. Their website is at:

www.brook.org.uk

Their confidential helpline can be contacted (Monday to Friday, 9 am–5 pm) at:

0800 0185 023

Movies

For some cultural bits and pieces that comment on adolescence and the problems that go with it, the movie *Donnie Darko* is an interesting and mind-bending piece; *Battle Royale* is a Japanese movie with some very interesting comments about the true nature of adolescence. Excellent fun is the *Buffy the Vampire Slayer* series, which addresses issues of friendship, the peer group, loss of virginity and what to do if your daughter's boyfriend is a 200-year-old vampire!